Marvelous Manhattan

Marvelous Manhattan

STORIES OF THE RESTAURANTS, BARS & SHOPS THAT MAKE THIS CITY SPECIAL

REGGIE NADELSON

ARTISAN | NEW YORK

Library of Congress Cataloging-in-Publication Data

Names: Nadelson, Reggie, author.
Title: Marvelous Manhattan / Reggie Nadelson.
Description: New York : Artisan, a division of Workman Publishing Co.,
    Inc. [2021]
Identifiers: LCCN 2020042971 | ISBN 9781579659790 (hardcover)
Subjects: LCSH: Nadelson, Reggie—Family. | Manhattan (New York,
    N.Y.)—Description and travel. | New York (N.Y.)—History—Anecdotes.
Classification: LCC F128.55 .N33 2021 | DDC 9174.7/104—dc23
LC record available at https://lccn.loc.gov/2020042971

Interior and jacket design by Nina Simoneaux
Cover lettering by Abraham Lule
Front jacket photograph copyright © by Mateusz Majewski/Unsplash

Artisan books are available at special discounts when purchased in bulk for premiums
and sales promotions as well as for fund-raising or educational use. Special editions or
book excerpts also can be created to specification. For details, contact the Special Sales
Director at the address below, or send an email to specialmarkets@workman.com.

For speaking engagements, contact speakersbureau@workman.com.

Published by Artisan
A division of Workman Publishing Co., Inc.
225 Varick Street
New York, NY 10014-4381
artisanbooks.com

Artisan is a registered trademark of Workman Publishing Co., Inc.

Published simultaneously in Canada by Thomas Allen & Son, Limited

Printed in China

First printing, March 2021

10 9 8 7 6 5 4 3 2 1

FOR LESLIE WOODHEAD,
A TRUE NEW YORKER

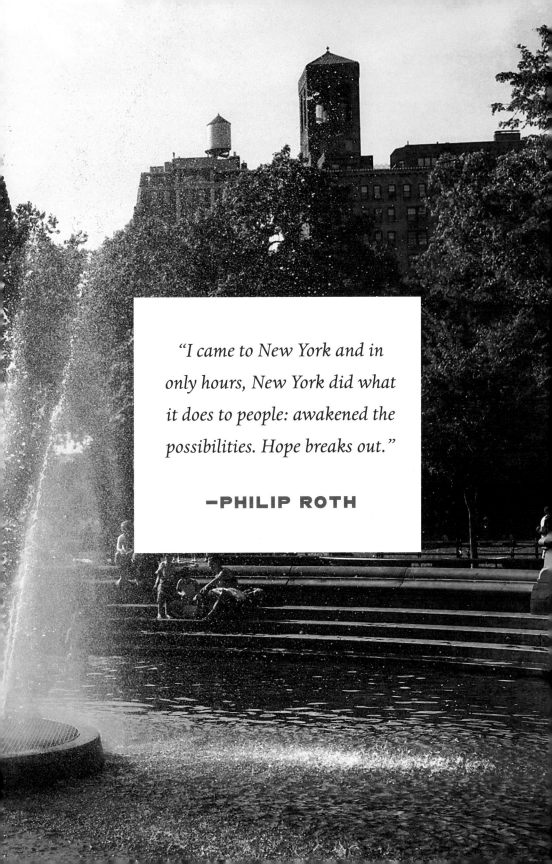

"I came to New York and in only hours, New York did what it does to people: awakened the possibilities. Hope breaks out."

–PHILIP ROTH

CONTENTS

LEFT TO RIGHT: My aunt Shirley Panzer; my mother,
Sally; and my godmother, Regina Senz, between
acts at the Met.

MY MOTHER'S NEW YORK

I N 1925, WHEN she was seventeen, my mother got the train from Winnipeg to New York.

"You hear that whistle, darling?" Sarah would say to her little sister, Jeanette. "That's the Canadian Pacific Railway, and one day I'm taking it to New York City." And she did, and almost from her arrival, the city was everything she had imagined.

In 1935, she filed naturalization papers that led to U.S. citizenship. In the document (where Sarah became Sally, a hipper, seemingly more urban moniker), as required, she forswore other allegiances, national or royal. In her heart, though, her true fealty was to New York City. She became one of E. B. White's "settlers."

In his 1949 book *Here Is New York*, the wonderful twentieth-century writer says that there are three New Yorks: "Commuters give the city its tidal restlessness; natives give it solidity and continuity; but the settlers give it passion." He adds that, of these three cities, "the greatest is the last—the city of final destination, the city that is a goal." The settler "embraces New York with the intense excitement of first love," and "absorbs New York with the fresh eyes of an adventurer."

My mother's fierce need to get to New York was driven by her ambition to become somebody else, to—like so many young women—live a freer, different life, away from the provinces, places of hidebound convention. New York appeared a shining city, flashing its lights shamelessly at you, a place where you could disappear, hide from your old self, create a new one.

As soon as she arrived, my mother joined the Communist Party and the Lucy Stone League, a group of early radical feminists. She shopped at Loehmann's, went to speakeasies like '21', to Connie's Inn in Harlem to see Louis Armstrong, to the Cherry Lane Theatre for avant-garde plays. "I remember your mother so well," says Jane Mushabac, my best friend in the Greenwich Village building where I grew up. "She had a mink coat, and your father wore a beret. She had been a Communist, which was fairly sophisticated; she drank martinis and was very stylish. Her favorite word was *stunning*, and she taught my mother about opera."

Stunning. My mother and her sister, who had moved to New York and was now calling herself Shirley, spoke to each other sometimes in Yiddish but more often using the hyperbolic lingo—stunning, divine, *marvelous*—of characters in a Noël Coward play (or Billy Crystal's homage to Fernando Lamas on *SNL*). To them, Manhattan was indeed marvelous. Many years later, Shirley, a newspaperwoman, would buy me my first martini at the Plaza.

It's 1939. Sally and my father, Sam, have moved to that Village apartment at 21 East 10th Street, where I would later be raised. Standing at the window in the new apartment, she looks across the street to the Hotel Albert café with its blinking red Eiffel Tower, then leans out as far as she can, takes note of the bars, galleries, bookshops, secondhand furniture stores, and of the skyline on the horizon. She felt then, as she always did, that New York was the gold ring.

For a couple of years now, I've been writing a column about the city for *T Magazine* at the *New York Times*. This book is based on those columns, but it's only now as I'm putting it together that I can see just how much my ma's feeling for the city rubbed off on me.

The column was given its title, The 212, by the writer Salman Rushdie, an old friend of mine and, like my mother, a settler. 212 was the original Manhattan area code. People hang on to it as if giving it up means losing some singular status. Very few cities cling to their myths or their history the way New York does; even as it hurries to tear things down, to build up bigger, higher, richer, there is always that rueful melancholy for the past.

In the *Times*, my column is described this way: "Reggie Nadelson revisits New York institutions that have defined cool for decades, from time-honored restaurants to unsung dives." Most of the places I love are one of a kind—independent bookshops, mom-and-pop cafés, corner bars. They are often run by second, third, fourth, even fifth generations of a family. At Schaller & Weber, Jeremy Schaller serves up great German sausage with his grandfather's passion for it. There is still good music at Minton's Playhouse in Harlem, where Thelonious Monk, Charlie Parker, and Dizzy Gillespie invented bebop in the 1940s. Niki Russ Federman is the fourth generation to run Russ & Daughters, the appetizing shop. After college, she went to work in the art world, but like her father, Mark Federman, she came back to Russ. Mark always says he heard "the call of the lox." "Time-honored," indeed.

"Unsung dives" are harder to find in a city where everyone is crazy to be first, to be in the know, to find that secret restaurant without a sign outside—like Indochine once was—indicating that if you can't find it, you don't belong. You imagine you've located a wonderful little-known Hungarian pastry shop near Columbia, only to hear from old friends that they frequented it in their college days.

"Cool" is something else. New York thinks it invented cool, although it was in fact Lester Young, the great saxophonist from Mississippi, who is thought to have originated the term around 1933, even before the Village Vanguard, where he played, opened.

My mother was pretty cool. She had unerring taste, though God knows where a girl from Winnipeg got it, how she knew where to shop in an age without internet. She worked as a nurse, but if a Chanel showed

up in the Back Room at the original Loehmann's in Brooklyn, she found it. She shopped at stores on University Place—grocer, fishmonger, shoemaker, florist (who is still there). She was friends with the bookseller on 10th Street, went for lunch alongside Village artists at the now long-gone counter at Bigelow's drugstore. I never asked her how she knew her way around. It was if she had a map of Manhattan imprinted on her heart. (I never asked anything much, for that matter, and that is part of the sadness of losing a parent; once the grief wears off, you feel a poignant sorrow that you never asked. You get the blues.)

Most of all, my mother understood that the city was all about the people, the connections that make New York sweet. This keeps loneliness at bay. If you only connect in New York, joy really does break out. That the maître d' at the Steak Joint knew my mother's name made her cool.

She made friends in Chinatown with the guy who had drawers crammed with "findings"—the minute stones that might have fallen out of your jewelry—and on the Lower East Side with the elderly Jewish guy who could restuff your pillows with goose down. Uptown, she had a special relationship with the shoe salesman at Delman's in Bergdorf Goodman, who saved the perfect pumps for her when they were on sale.

My mother loved the city she got familiar with over the decades, but she was also always on the hunt for the new, and she haunted the

My father, Sam, smoking his pipe on our terrace overlooking Washington Square Park.

Museum of Modern Art when it could still shock. She understood that this city in a hurry, in pursuit of a buck, of the most avant-garde, was most of all about change. So on Saturday afternoons in SoHo, where I now live, when the tourists line up for weird $600 sneakers, or when the Whitney Museum moves downtown, or my favorite diner gives up the ghost, I think of my mother and remind myself that all this is New York, too. I remind myself that the new also includes the likes of the fabulous High Line.

My parents took pleasure in the city, but in a sense, they earned it, because they toughed it out. My father grew up on the Lower East Side in the early twentieth century, when it was the worst slum in the world. They got through two world wars, the Spanish influenza, the Great Depression, polio, Joe McCarthy, the Cuban Missile Crisis, the Mad Bomber, and Son of Sam. We all got through the crime waves of the 1970s. I was here for 9/11, the Great Recession of 2008, and Superstorm Sandy.

Which inevitably brings me to the coronavirus pandemic and how it revealed so much about the city. As the lockdown began, I watched SoHo residents clear the shelves of groceries, pack up their Mercs and Jeeps, and head for the Hamptons or the Hudson Valley. My fellow stalwart New Yorkers and I saw them go and, with a certain bravado, thought: *Bye-bye. More space for us.* Friends who were leaving town said, "What's the point of New York anyhow if there's no theater, no art cinemas, no opera, no jazz clubs, no restaurants?"

I thought: *If you don't know the point, it's best you go. You're no settler.*

The harsh reality of the coronavirus is that people got brutally sick, or died, and in some cases lost their homes and went hungry. I was lucky. Gourmet Garage delivered. Thompson Chemists called all its regulars to make sure they had enough meds for the duration. Russ & Daughters delivered lox. Davide Drummond biked six miles to and from Brooklyn to make sure his West Broadway coffee shop, Ground Support Café, stayed open, that the residents of SoHo had their caffeine and maybe an almond croissant.

Many restaurants did eventually open outdoors, and this has turned the whole city into a version of a Parisian café, only better—because it's in New York. After months of lockdown, the first meal I had out with a friend was at Fanelli's, where they had put a couple of tables on the street. I had a BLT, and it was the best meal I'd ever eaten. Neighbors passed by. The city seemed to breathe and stretch. And we knew it would be okay. Somehow. Astonishingly, all the places I had planned to put in this book a year ago are still here. We are still here.

My mother felt that life would not be much worth living without New York City. I think she might have been right. Or, as John Updike wrote, "The true New Yorker secretly believes that people living any-where else have to be, in some sense, kidding."

Of the pieces here, some were originally published in a different form in *T Magazine*. The places I write about here run roughly from south to north in Manhattan. Inevitably a lot of them are downtown, but then that's where, one way and another, I've lived my whole life.

The front door of my building in SoHo. It was designed by Henry Fernbach, New York's first prominent Jewish architect, in 1881, in the Neo-Grec manner.

RUSS & DAUGHTERS

LOX ET VERITAS" is one of the slogans on the walls inside Russ & Daughters, along with old signs advertising lake sturgeon. The slogan is, of course, a joke, but then laughter is high on the list of nutrients you get from eating Jewish: comedy, history, nostalgia.

It's on a cold December morning that I'm sitting outside the Russ shop on East Houston Street eating a hot latke; this little pancake is made of grated potato and onion, fried golden brown, eaten with sour cream or crème fraîche, applesauce, a nice spoonful of red caviar—the fat red salmon roe that you can pop with your tongue. Most often, latkes are eaten to celebrate Hanukkah, which is next week, though it would be a sorry thing to relegate them to one holiday.

I used to come down to Russ with my pop for lox and bagels. I like to think it was usually on Saturday night, so we'd have the good stuff for

Founder Joel Russ with his daughters—
from left to right, Anne, Hattie, and Ida—
in the 1950s.

breakfast on Sunday, but the truth is, I can't really remember. Still, I sit with the latke as if it will remind me, as if it were my Proustian nosh.

So much of my life is invested in this little shop on the Lower East Side that's a few blocks from where my father was born and grew up. Sitting here, I feel the weight of all this history. History. Reality. Myth. The New York trilogy. Over a century ago, as a kid, my pop was probably eyeing a plump schmaltz herring or a pickle at Joel Russ's first shop, which opened on Orchard Street in 1914. A few years later, the store moved here, to 179 East Houston.

Mr. Russ had no sons. His three daughters, who had worked in the store for years, eventually took over the business, and one of them, Anne, begat Mark and his sister, Tara; and Mark begat Niki, and Tara begat Josh. These days, Niki Russ Federman co-owns the store with Josh Russ Tupper, her first cousin. They opened the Russ Café on Orchard Street in 2014, and a year later, another one at the Jewish Museum on the Upper East Side.

On the front of the Houston Street shop is a pink-and-green neon sign with two little lox next to the lettering. Outside, a line has formed. A whole new generation has discovered the shop, and if you are a real Russ-nik, you wait. After all, inside is Paradise.

Fourth-generation Russes and current owners Josh Russ Tupper and Niki Russ Federman.

To your left as you enter is a counter that runs the length of the store. Here is the shining pink smoked salmon, the fatty, salty cured belly lox that, with cream cheese on a bagel, gave its name to the greatest sandwich ever produced by humankind. This is a fine thing anywhere, but at Russ, it is the most marvelous, especially if you get it with the more expensive, less salty, la-di-da Nova.

Other kinds of smoked salmon are arrayed in one of the glass cases, too, a United Nations of salmon: the salmon from Nova Scotia, of course, and also from Norway, Scotland, and Ireland, as well as Western wild salmon. And there's smoked sturgeon, creamy, expensive, and rich; smoked sable (black cod); and those little golden-skinned chub and baby-size whitefish—not to mention caviars pricier than the 24 karat stuff, and the less-exalted roes: black, red, and the grass-green roe of tiny flying fish. Vats of various cream cheeses: scallion, caviar, vegetable; and the herring in cream sauce, and in wine sauce; the chopped herring salad; and fresh herring from Holland when they come in (oh, the Holland herring), or French herring if you're fancy. And latkes, now available year-round.

Half a dozen slicers and servers are working. White coats on, they look up to answer questions and take orders, and if they recognize a regular, there's an exchange about kids and family. Chhapte Sherpa, born in the Eastern Himalayas, used to tell everyone that his New York name was Sherpa Lox and that he was from KatmanJew. This was a guy who guided people to Everest Base Camp once upon a time and in the aftermath of Superstorm Sandy easily ran up twelve flights to deliver food to people who were stranded. In 2020, sadly, Sherpa died. But I'll never forget our delicious conversations.

"Sandwich?" he'd ask.

"Half," I'd say. "I already ate a latke."

"A bissel butter?" (At Russ, you can have an order of cream cheese or whitefish salad or almost anything in three sizes: a quart, a pint, or, if you only want a little bite, a smidge, a taste, a bissel.) Sherpa would make my bespoke sandwich, a lightly buttered toasted bialy with smoked sturgeon and smoked salmon. Meanwhile, he'd tell me about his kids' progress at school. Nearly the best part of a visit to Russ—well, not quite as good as the reserve smoked sturgeon—has always been the socializing.

You go in before a holiday, any holiday, and the place is packed with people and their parents and their kids, and maybe "kids" who are now grandparents themselves. You wait for your order; you kibitz relentlessly. Mark Federman, Niki's father, who quit his law practice to take up with the lox racket and ran the place for years with his wife, Maria, was a grade A schmoozer, and a lovely guy; he still is. Niki and Josh are coming along nicely in this art form.

Opposite the fish counter near the front of the store are piles of dried fruits—apricots, pineapple, dates, pears, papaya—glistening like jewels.

RUSS & DAUGHTERS
APPETIZERS
179
RUSS & DAUGHTERS
DELIVERS
GASTROPOLIS

Glass jars contain chocolate-covered jellies, and three kinds of halvah, and doughnuts for Hanukkah. Also, the rugelach, the salted caramel macaroons, the black-and-white cookies, the cinnamon babka, the chocolate babka. All of it baked now at the new Russ facility in the Brooklyn Navy Yard, a place so big and white, clean, and fragrant that Joel Russ would surely have imagined he was in heaven.

"One for the road," says Josh, holding up a golden bagel he has plucked from a small mountain of bialys and bagels. The Russ bagel, also baked at the Navy Yard, is possibly the best in town. This is a great bagel, a Nobel Prize–worthy bagel, glistening and crusty, hard but chewy; a bagel that's like life.

Bagels, bialys, babka (all three good toasted with a schmear); shopping bags; and, in the far-left corner, the alluring blue caviar tins, promising ecstasy.

People come here because it reminds them of their past, their history, their dreams. On the wall at the back are family photographs, evocative black-and-white pictures from across the twentieth century, of Mr. Russ and the three daughters, and their children. These photos prod my own memories and probably those of a lot of other customers; for one friend, at least, the pictures on the wall are his "Rosebud." Our own grandparents and great-grandparents, most of whom came from eastern Europe, show up in family pictures not unlike those on the walls of the Russ shop. In a way, Russ has given me a sense of my own past, even of my own Jewishness, a very particular kind of secular New York Jewishness—and a desire to reclaim it.

"Food is one of the deepest ways we have to connect to and take pride in who we are," says Niki.

"Russ brings back memories people wish they had of a time when shopping meant you knew the butcher, the grocer, the fish guy, and the pickle man, and each shop was its own tiny community, where people knew your name," says Mark.

During the coronavirus lockdown, I called to order a delivery. I got Johanna Shipman, the store manager who was working at the Navy Yard production center. I asked her if she was anxious about the staff, and about herself. "I worry about everyone, of course," she said, "but I worry, too, about the continuity of Russ & Daughters and the things that matter in the city and make it worth living in."

KATZ'S DELICATESSEN

Katz's Delicatessen is immense, and the lighting is not kind. But you don't come for your close-up, so you take your ticket and a tray and head for the counter, where the guys will hack off pastrami with exquisite precision, piling it up on rye. Or you spend a few bucks for waiter service and settle in at a table against the wall under a million celebrity photographs.

Katz's opened in 1888 (under the name Iceland Brothers), and it was renamed and moved to its current location, at the corner of East Houston and Ludlow, in 1910.

Many decades later, it was, of course, the place where, in *When Harry Met Sally . . .*, Meg Ryan faked the noisy orgasm to prove to Billy Crystal that women can do it. A customer at the next table (played by Estelle Reiner, director Rob Reiner's mother), memorably says, "I'll have what she's having."

At Katz's, the pastrami is very nice, rich, luscious purply meat. There's other great stuff—knishes, kugel, salami. (Katz's salami became famous during World War II thanks to their slogan "Send a Salami to Your Boy in the Army.") If you want to die in a heavenly sort of way, order a meat platter with everything: pastrami, corned beef, salami, pickles, potato salad, stacks of rye bread. Whatever you want.

But I come for the tongue. I love tongue. (Even after visiting a meat-processing plant in southern Kansas where I saw tongues that had been newly removed from the cattle tossed in a canvas bucket, I still love it.) My father liked it scrambled with eggs. Me, I'm a purist. I'll take a plate of sliced tongue, maybe a little coleslaw and pickles, a slice or two of rye, plenty of mustard.

ECONOMY CANDY

Mitchell Cohen was five when his pop, Morris "Moise" Cohen (whose father had started the business), stood him on a milk crate at Economy Candy to work the cash register. From such little boys grow the guys who, like Mitchell, go to Wharton and then Goldman Sachs. Eventually he figured candy was more fun and took over the shop on Rivington Street, where he sells every candy bar you've ever heard of, along with Pez

dispensers and rock candy swizzle sticks. M&Ms in every color; gummy bears and fish, gummy sushi and pizzas; enormous gumballs in purple and orange and lime green. Nuts, too, and fancy chocolates as well as old-timey candy bars. The small shop is filled, packed, jammed floor to ceiling with sweets.

What Mitchell and his wife, Skye, sell most of all is the nostalgia induced when you set your eyes on Goobers and Raisinets, Black Cows and Turkish Taffy. (Alas, no Reggie! Bar remains anywhere; named for Reggie Jackson, Mr. October, it's my favorite, naturally—nobody ever names anything Reggie.)

There is also nostalgia here for the out-of-town shopper, including the legendary Australia Violet Crumble Bar and British sweeties that run to Bounty, Aero, Maltesers, and the "authentic" Mars bars.

In 1912, when my pop was a kid and living around here, the cool candy was Life Savers, so named because they resembled life preservers. Maybe in a sense they were. For a kid who grew up poor on the Lower East Side, candy, if you could get any at all, was a sweet moment in a grim universe.

THE TENEMENT MUSEUM

In the late 1880s, my father's parents and older brothers came by ship to Ellis Island, fleeing the shtetl where they lived in the Pale of Settlement (a long stretch of Russia, Poland, and Ukraine). Born in New York City, my pa grew up in a tenement not far from Orchard Street, in what was then the biggest and worst slum anywhere. His story is like that of millions of others, Jews who had come from eastern Europe crammed into the Lower East Side, and I went to the Tenement Museum thinking I'd get a look at what it was like.

The old building has rooms and apartments done up as they were in those years around the turn of the twentieth century. The period furnishings are quaint, the rooms clean, the floors polished. It's very well done except for the smell; it doesn't smell of anything. My father grew up in a building like this, and in his telling, the stink was unimaginable.

Whole families shared a single room. It was excruciatingly hot in the summer, freezing in winter, and everyone, including little kids, worked for twelve, fourteen hours a day, seven days a week. Families who couldn't pay the rent, often widowed women with kids, were kicked out onto the street. Tuberculosis and cholera were rampant, and hunger was pervasive; people starved to death.

My father, like many in his generation, trying to protect us kids from the unspeakable facts of his early life, almost never talked about it—except once. He told me the story of a family in his building that didn't have enough food for all six children. A decision had to be made: which child would be allowed to die, and given a rag dipped in sugar water to keep her calm.

Hard to believe with all the snazzy cafés and cool young people, and even the delightful shop at the Tenement Museum itself, with its good book selection and retro alarm clocks, that this was a terrifying slum. Hard to understand what it would have been like, the horrendous stink, the horror, the disease and despair that Jacob Riis described in his book *How the Other Half Lives* (available at the museum shop).

——

JING FONG

T'S THE LURE of lovely, luscious shrimp dumplings for breakfast that calls me to Chinatown at 9:30 on certain Saturday mornings. This is not crazy. These are the best shrimp dumplings in Manhattan, succulent, with the outer layer—the pleated dough—thin and fragile, a modest, tender wrapper.

Most of the customers are regulars, the anticipation showing on their faces. My friend Dawn Delbanco, a Chinese Chinese art professor, is with me on a recent visit. She is a woman who knows her dumplings. "Dumplings are a type of dim sum," she explains. "'Dim sum' just means 'a dot' or 'a little bit of heart.'"

We go early because within an hour, there will be a line snaking down Elizabeth Street as far as Canal, customers inspecting the numbers they've been given, eagerly awaiting the sticky rice in lotus leaves, the fish balls and shrimp balls, the spring rolls and steamed spareribs. Shrimp and spinach dumplings, too, and panfried shrimp and chive ones, baked green bean pastry puffs, turnip cake, taro cake, and maybe a cold beer—which goes best with this food, even at breakfast.

We're in. Whisked up by the steep escalator to the third floor, where the vast restaurant—18,000 square feet, all red and gold and glittering chandeliers—seats eight hundred. There are older dumpling parlors in Manhattan's Chinatown, including at least one that's been made to look "retro"; for me, though, none is better than Jing Fong. And for Dawn, none more completely evokes the Hong Kong dim sum palaces of her childhood. Jing Fong is very, very noisy.

Dawn's parents were from Hong Kong, and she often visited the island with them as a child. There the dim sum parlors were filled with "earsplitting noise," she recalls, adding, "The Cantonese are not soft-spoken, and there would be dozens of young women with trays of food weighing perhaps fifty pounds carried on a strap around their shoulders yelling out the offerings. The families were all yelling, too."

"You could taste that noise," she says over breakfast, examining the delicacies as the food carts fly by, each bearing half a dozen wicker baskets containing dim sum and other dishes.

If Jing Fong is much admired for its dim sum, it is also part of the modern history of Manhattan's Chinatown. When the restaurant opened at 24 Elizabeth Street in 1978, it had only 150 seats. Its early years seem tangled up in fact and lore, lawsuits and union problems and worse, in what was then a city bleeding from crime. The gang violence in Chinatown was bad, and it was lousy for business; centered on Doyers Street, it spilled over into the whole of the neighborhood. Although there's a certain nostalgia for the New York of the 1970s (okay, the music was good), it was a miserable, murderous time.

Jing Fong, which translates from the Cantonese as "golden wind," was simply a name the original owners came up with—perhaps because it had good feng shui, suggests Claudia Leo, one of the restaurant's executives. In the '70s, everyone in Chinatown needed some luck.

The original owner of Jing Fong eventually went bankrupt and was rescued by the Lam family, beginning with Shui Ling Lam (known as Grandpa Lam). A master plumber, he bought the majority share of the

Saturday brunch crowds lining up (left) and heading up to mecca (right).

restaurant and, in 1993, moved it next door to its current location at 20 Elizabeth Street. Grandpa Lam passed the restaurant to his son, Ming; then Ming Lam's son, Truman, came into the business, and it's now a thorough-going family affair.

A good-looking, hip, slightly shy guy, Truman is the only member of the third generation of Lams to work at Jing Fong. He went to NYU, then worked in investment banking, but when his parents took over Jing Fong from his grandfather, his mother asked him to help modernize the computer system. "I got sucked in," says Truman, adding, "This is way more stressful than investment banking, where you work maybe sixty-plus hours a week but the worst-case scenario is you get fired. We have 180 staff, 140 full-time, and if something happens, it's you who fixes it."

The changing patterns of Chinese immigration also worry Truman. The trend is for newly arriving Chinese, he notes, to go to Sunset Park in Brooklyn or Flushing in Queens. And there are hard-core foodies who insist that there are dim sum joints in the boroughs as good as or better than Jing Fong. But Truman is a steadfast Manhattanite, who rides his bike to work from his home in Battery Park City.

Dim sum ladies pitching
their wares.

I've been eating in Manhattan's Chinatown all my life. I like to stroll downtown from Greenwich Village, where I grew up, first to the Jewish neighborhood (lox, knishes), then on to Little Italy (fresh mozzarella, cannoli) and Chinatown. To me, dim sum are best eaten

Third-generation owner Truman Lam and executive dim sum chef Jin Ruan having a laugh in the kitchen.

with family and a load of friends and sprinkled with soy sauce. Of the old downtown neighborhoods, Chinatown is the only one that has really grown over the years, as Little Italy has retreated to just a few blocks around Grand Street. Plunge into Bayard and Pell Streets on a weekday, lose yourself among the local ladies shopping for groceries, and buy a bag of fresh lychees, and you feel you're adrift on another continent.

My greatest success in restaurant-going, my one true moment of celebrity, took place at Jing Fong on Christmas Day. Traditionally, New York Jews ate Chinese food on Christmas because nothing much else was open. Even now, when there is plenty of choice, a lot of us still want Chinese food on December 25. Last year, my friend Didi and her family and I showed up at Jing Fong around eleven in the morning. The woman at the door was already furiously shooing people away. Every table was full. She did not look happy to see us approach, but when I gave my name, she looked down at something written in Chinese characters and beamed. Claudia Leo had booked a table for us. As we were swept upstairs, Didi burst out laughing. To be known at Jing Fong is to have made it in New York City, she said: "You have finally arrived!"

But back to my morning with Dawn. Jing Fong is filling up; it's packed with families, grandmas, couples, teenagers, kids. As the noise grows, tables are covered with baskets and platters of noodles, including beef chow fun; dumplings that have been steamed, fried, panfried; squid; turnip cakes; egg custard buns; cups of tea; cans of Coke; bottles of beer. Truman, who joins us, nibbles steamed spareribs. He recalls that when his family lived on Long Island, he loved coming for brunch because he'd see all his cousins and they could fool around.

There is also a buffet spread with myriad hot dishes. More and more carts of dim sum fly by, seemingly faster and faster, as if on a Formula One course. Dawn is watching closely for the har gow, the shrimp dumplings served in a woven bamboo basket.

Har gow is the standard by which all dumplings are judged, and they are the great test of a dim sum chef, she says. The rice-flour wrapping, sometimes called a shrimp bonnet, has to be delicate, transparent, and smooth except for as many as ten tiny pleats. The skin must not break when you pick up the dumpling. It must be light, the shrimp filling just enough for a single perfect bite. Dawn picks one up with her chopsticks. Eats. With a certainty born of those many trips to Hong Kong on her face, she says emphatically, "These dumplings are very good."

DI PALO'S

ON A BALMY fall day on the slopes of Mount Etna, as a breeze rustles through the grapevines, Lou Di Palo talks about his Sicilian ancestors. Three or four times a year, Lou takes a small group to Italy to learn about regional food and wine and, most important, meet the people and sample their specialties. In a vineyard here, we're drinking a local red wine and listening to Lou, in his usual black jeans and shirt, talk about how it is partly because of this wild, elusive countryside that he's now in New York running his legendary shop. A terrible volcanic eruption wiped out the holdings of one of his ancestors and forced the family to emigrate. Now Lou is back in Sicily for a few weeks. A history buff, he is also passionate about the local wines and food, a connoisseur and an evangelist.

Between 1880 and 1930, more than a million Sicilians migrated to America—many of them to what is still known as Little Italy in downtown New York City. Along with his Sicilian ancestors, Lou counts family from Lucania (in the instep of the Italian boot). Five generations later at his great gourmet shop on Grand Street, he sells Italy's best cheeses, meats, olive oils, and wines.

Giorgio DeLuca (center), cofounder of the gourmet store Dean & DeLuca, shopping for cheese.

Lou is New York's patron saint of Italy's gourmet delicacies. Critic, epicure, author, he lectures on wine and olive oil from a profound store of knowledge. Still, most days, he's behind the counter at the shop, slicing the silky San Daniele ham, selling the freshly made mozzarella that's still warm and dripping from the Di Palo kitchen, and schmoozing (what's Italian for schmoozing?) with customers.

This has been a family shop for more than a hundred years. As usual, Lou's sister Marie and her daughter Jessica are also here—stopping from time to time to exchange a mother-daughter smile—and so is his brother Sal, who will entertain you with the best bad jokes in downtown Manhattan.

Sam Di Palo, home on furlough from the army,
with his mother, Concetta.

Savino (Sam) Di Palo, the current
owners' father, outside the shop, 1948.

Walking south on Mott Street to Di Palo's, I always hear Ella Fitzgerald singing "Manhattan" with its sweetly ironic Lorenz Hart lyrics: "What street compares with Mott Street in July? Sweet pushcarts gliding by."

No pushcarts on Mott now. But according to Lou, the street was jammed with them when his great-grandfather Savino Di Palo, who had been a farmer and cheese maker in Italy, arrived in New York and in 1910 opened a tiny dairy at 131 Mott.

In the glass cases under the counters and in the refrigerated cabinets behind them is an astonishing array of wonderful Italian cheeses (my favorite, a pungent blue with a rind made of cranberries soaked in port), cured meats (I love the mortadella with pistachios), prepared foods that might include eggplant parm, meatballs in a rich tomato sauce, or just-made porchetta, its rings of fat crackling and brown with heat and flavor. There is bright-green broccoli rabe, olives and sun-dried tomatoes and roasted red peppers, and pasta. On the shelves are Italian groceries— jams, honey, cookies, small-batch olive oils, and great balsamic vinegar, some of it as expensive as good Cognac and a glorious addition to the little wild strawberries the Italians call fragoline.

"I always feel better when I come here early," says one woman at the shop, inhaling the scent of a sheer slice of pink prosciutto as if it were oxygen. "This is like breakfast but better," says her friend, who is working on a crumbly piece of the new spring Parmigiano aged in hay. Food writer Ruth Reichl considers the Parmigiano the best in town, and she notes that it sells at a very good price. Di Palo's is Ruth's "favorite shop in the world," she says—not a bad recommendation.

The two women, perhaps in their seventies, continue to sample the hams, the sopressata, even a tiny curl of lardo. A long line forms—locals, tourists, an Italian comic who entertains the room. One young woman, though, is furious; she only wants a sandwich, she doesn't want to wait, she doesn't get it. Kind but firm, Lou says to her, "That's not how we do things here." Here you need time to sample, to chat, to joke around. This has been going on for decades; Di Palo's has survived the complainers for a long, long time.

In New York, where we whine and moan, kvetch and groan every time something is torn down but are equally irritated when something loses its edge, Di Palo's is one of the few institutions that seems delicately balanced between past and present; with deep roots, it embraces old and new, especially with the young generation getting into the business. Next door, Lou's daughter oversees the wine shop the family owns; around the corner, his son is setting up a new osteria.

At the osteria, you can drink wine, nibble cheese, and attend events about Italian food and wine. I've been coming to Di Palo's all my life, and I rarely make it out of the store without biting into the mozzarella made there, the milk dripping down my chin. Maybe now I can sit down to eat it.

The new space is elegant, cool, and sleekly designed. With its Carrara marble counter, slate floors, and cream leather banquettes, it resembles the set of an Italian film. A kind of back-to-the-future outpost, it seems to be the family's way of staying Italian into the twenty-first century.

In for a look at the osteria, Linda Schulze, a longtime customer and neighbor (her husband, photographer

Co-owners Lou Di Palo, contemplating cheese behind the counter, and his sister Marie Di Palo, laughing in the background.

John Matturri, bought their loft here in 1979), says, "You just can't get this food anywhere else. If Di Palo's ever leaves the neighborhood, we leave the neighborhood."

Jessica, a fifth-generation Di Palo who, along with her cousins, has studied in Italy, says, "Over the last decade, my generation started to understand the potential around us within the family business and the changing neighborhood. We want to maintain tradition with a new trend, to relate the story to a new generation."

Di Palo's has come full circle. When Savino came to America, he spoke no Italian, only a regional dialect. The fifth generation, Americans with graduate degrees, have all learned Italian; it will be up to them to keep the culture alive. In 1950, half of Little Italy was Italian; by 2000, it was down to 6 percent. For Di Palo's and the few remaining authentic shops around Grand and Mulberry, it's almost a mission to keep the culinary traditions alive. For the family, Italian food and wine are art and history.

Squint a little on Mott Street—or rent the movie—and you can see Marlon Brando as the Godfather buying oranges in front of 131, the original Di Palo's. Lou's mother was making the mozzarella when, as she told him, some unkempt guy came in. She knew he was from the film crew, so she wiped her hands on her apron and told him there was a lot of detail that was wrong and he should change it. Lou recalls, "I said to her, 'Ma, do you know who that was?'" Turned out it was Francis Ford Coppola, who became a fan and a customer.

"People ask me why you can't order from Di Palo's online," says Lou. "A young man came in and said, 'I get everything on Amazon; why can't I get Di Palo's things?' I said to him, 'You can't get history or flavor or the particular something that comes from conversation with five generations online.'"

GEORGE WASHINGTON
DRANK HERE

——

THE EAR INN

THERE ARE GHOSTS at 326 Spring Street. This two-hundred-plus-year-old building, now home to the Ear Inn, has been frequented by the Portuguese and Dutch sailors who arrived in the earliest days of white men on Manhattan; by the sailors and passengers who came through this well-trafficked waterfront in the late nineteenth century, looking for a drink; and by the dockworkers and longshoremen of the mid-twentieth century.

You can hear the ghosts when the band plays on Sunday nights; they seem to rattle the whole building. Some people think it's just the vibrations from the music, but others know the truth. The place vibrates with New York history, with the thrilling story of a city becoming itself.

In the apartment upstairs, a collection of old Dutch gin jugs shudders, Champagne bottles made of thick ancient glass rattle, and

apothecary flasks from the eighteenth century clink against each other. The building has housed a bar continuously since 1817. In those days, water literally lapped at the building, which was then just four feet from the Hudson River.

The Earregulars, the house jazz band, playing a Sunday night gig.

Back then, this area was still part of the pastoral exurban village of Greenwich, which had been left off the grid the city fathers laid out for Manhattan in 1811. (Thus, anything unconventional would be labeled "off the grid.") But Greenwich was incorporated into the city of New York in 1817—the same year construction began on the Erie Canal, which would soon make the port of New York explode with produce from the American heartland carried to the city and sent abroad, and imports from Europe shipped out into the Midwest. "Even in my time, you could still smell the coffee and the spices from the ships," says Rip Hayman (that's Captain Richard Perry Hayman, of the US Merchant Marine), who now co-owns the Ear with Martin Sheridan.

Hayman and Sheridan bought the joint in the 1970s and have coddled it, repaired it, and lavished love and affection on it ever since. When they arrived, the Ear was still a longshoremen's dive where the guys who didn't get a gig unloading ships (see *On the Waterfront*) drank at the bar

Ancient Dutch glass gin bottles, dug up from the foundations of the bar.

Memorabilia on the wall at the Ear.

from five in the morning until noon. They were plenty pissed off when Sheridan and Hayman, two young, educated middle-class guys, tossed the pool table and the jukebox and changed the Ear's MO, adding food and civility. For a while, a faint threat of class warfare hung in the air.

These days, you walk in and you're like Alice, falling down the rabbit hole into New York's past. The ceilings are low. The wood is old. Up front is the bar itself, its back wall swamped by old bottles and jugs. Memorabilia cling like barnacles to the Ear's walls. A variety of beers and ales, enough to satisfy any beer bore, are displayed. There are tables, too, and a back room where you can linger and eat the best dumplings this side of Chinatown. "We've been coming to the Ear for years," a local says. "I love it because you go in and it looks like a scene, you know, too cool for school, but then you get in back and everyone is welcoming like they've always been and the Chinese chef is whipping up something delicious."

Waves of customers come and go throughout the day; first, for lunch, are the editors from a nearby publishing house and the tourists. A woman perusing a guidebook says with a German accent, "My book says this is the last real place in New York."

Then comes the cocktail crowd, the groups of twenty-somethings who gather on the sidewalk in good weather, and the residents of the

The bar in the 1950s,
before bits of the "B" came
off, and Bar became Ear.

shiny new condos. "It's all dog walkers and joggers around here now,"
says Hayman. "You can smell the Botox in the evening," he adds with
very benign sarcasm.

In his lilting Irish accent, Sheridan says that during Fashion Week,
with shows nearby, "Models wandered past looking like lost gorgeous
peacocks on their high heels. You'd think they'd have more sense." The
guys might complain, but they love it all.

Strange name for a bar, the Ear Inn. The red neon sign outside is
from the 1930s, after Prohibition, Hayman believes. The Landmarks
Preservation Commission refused any additions to its design but had no
problem with a subtraction and so, voilà, "Bar" became "Ear." The sign
became a kind of beacon, a lighthouse lamp in what was then a desolate corner of the city where the homeless warmed themselves at barrel
fires. "I used to bring them sacks of potatoes for roasting," says Sheridan.
Over lunch—creamy soup, great cheeseburgers, Guinness for Sheridan,
Gooseneck IPA for Hayman—the two recall their early days at the Ear,
when there were still artists and writers in downtown Manhattan. John
Lennon hung out at the bar. Allen Ginsburg recited "Howl." Artist Sari
Dienes lived upstairs; when Hayman wanted to buy the Ear, she sold a
Rauschenberg she owned to help him purchase it.

Fast-forward to 2006, when construction on the glass box condo next to the Ear began and the foundations of the old building were dug up and stabilized. "Finds included apothecary bottles for elixirs and salves," says Hayman. "They dug down about six feet and got pieces of the actual original pier into the Hudson, animal skeletons, those Champagne bottles from the Dutch period, because the Dutch drank Champagne with their oysters," he says. Adds Sheridan, "The New-York Historical Society, when we gave them everything, said it was the best find in one hundred years."

The Ear is sometimes known as the James Brown House. Brown was an aide to George Washington, whose estate was down the road from the Ear. It is sometimes said that Brown is the Black man depicted in Emanuel Leutze's legendary, if apocryphal, painting *Washington Crossing the Delaware*. Brown had this house built for himself in the 1770s, and he lived there as a prosperous tobacconist and apothecary until his death.

Around 1985 or so, the other James Brown was in town, playing Madison Square Garden, and the Ear's owners invited him to the bar. Sheridan says a message came back: "Brown said he couldn't come, and also that the fried chicken in New York was so bad, he was going back to Georgia."

Sheridan swears that both James Brown stories are true, more or less; I believe it all. The Ear is that kind of place. Anyway, why let facts get in the way of a great tale? Cue the storytelling; wake the ghosts.

THOMPSON CHEMISTS

I **N HIS BOOK** *A Walker in the City,* Alfred Kazin writes, "It is the old drugstore I miss the most. . . . Once it was the most exciting threshold I had ever crossed. In the windows glass urns of rose- and pink- and blue-colored water hung from chains."

To real New Yorkers, the drugstore has always been an essential part of neighborhood life. When I was growing up, Romanoff Pharmacy on the corner of University Place and 10th Street was our drugstore. It had a soda fountain, a row of phone booths, a door that led into the lobby of our building, and displays of Revlon nail polish (Fire & Ice for my mother) and Whitman's Samplers, those fancy yellow boxes of chocolates. The druggist (that was what we called the pharmacist) was discreet and made sure that buying your first box of Tampax was not a public event.

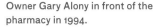

Owner Gary Alony in front of the   Gary and his wife and business partner,
pharmacy in 1994.   Jolie—still in love after all these years.

Thompson Chemists is SoHo's corner drugstore, where people like me who live in the neighborhood go for their prescriptions and to buy salves and potions, ointments and lotions, and Italian toothpaste. The UPS guy is usually offered a cold Coke. The kid who draws hearts on the pavement comes by for his stipend of colored chalk—he's aiming for ten thousand hearts for peace and love.

The store caters to the last remaining Italian workingpeople in the area and to the new SoHo residents who want imported shampoo and rare skin creams. It has these, but it also has something better: It has Gary. Gary Alony, the co-owner with his wife, Jolie, is SoHo's pharmacist—and much more.

In its current logo, Thompson Chemists announces itself as an alchemist, which implies that they make magic. Gary and Jolie do just that in the little community center they've woven around the shop. Regulars come and go or just hang out for a while. Patti Smith is a friend; so is Whoopi Goldberg. People call about a sore throat or a reaction to antibiotics. Gary is the kind of pharmacist who, if he notices an older customer with badly swollen ankles, gently suggests a visit to the clinic. During the coronavirus pandemic, he called every regular to make sure they had all the medications they needed.

For Gary, a neighborhood drugstore is a sacred thing, and he's there if your kid has scraped their knee or if, like a fool (me, in other words), you've tripped on some broken pavement and fallen flat on your face. More humiliated than hurt (the worst part of falling, if you don't die, is that so many people stop to help, or tourists to take your picture!), I hightailed it to Thompson Chemists, where the family dog, Rego, was, as usual, lying on the floor. Gary gave me an enormous ice pack and checked for a concussion. Jolie handed me some magnesium and ordered lunch for all of us.

But then, Gary comes from a family of healers; displayed on a shelf is the brass mortar and pestle that belonged to his Yemenite Israeli great-grandmother. His grandmother who lived in Queens, where Gary grew up, always said to him, "You're born into this world to make things better; this is the point of our existence, to help without expectation of anything."

Suspended from the ceiling are large, soft, very witty sculptures of the couple made by their late friend the artist Ed Fenner. Jolie, who grew up partly in France and speaks five languages, is vivacious and available to all who show up for advice and conversation.

There's always music on in the store—Gary is a fan of folk, blue-grass, country, rock. Twice a month, usually on a Wednesday evening, there's live music. Sheriff Bob Saidenberg sets up in front of the shelves of Lipitor and Advil, La Roche and Marvis, and Thompson Chemists' own brand of candles and bath salts, which Gary makes in his kitchen at home. "Where it's dark as a dungeon, damp as the dew," Bob and his group sing. Bob does folk and country, as well as bluegrass, and standing among a group of locals, I sing along: "Danger is double, pleasures are few . . . it's dark as a dungeon way down in the mines." SoHo neighbors pop in, listen, clap; little kids race around the shop; Jolie hands out candy.

If Gary could, he'd have an old-fashioned soda fountain on Thompson Street, for in his eyes, the drugstore is as central to life here as it would be in any small town. This neighborhood *is* our town, the drugstore as beloved and cherished as anything in a Thornton Wilder play.

In spite of all its magic, the future of Thompson Chemists is always in question. People say they love old-fashioned stores, but they shop at CVS because it's a few cents cheaper. Most people in SoHo can afford more than a few cents; maybe you get the city you pay for.

Gary looks out at a perfect storm of greed and monopoly, of big drugstore chains, Big Pharma, big insurance companies that fish out and kill independent drugstores, and says ruefully, "I hope people give their neighborhood stores a chance instead of looking back years later and saying, 'Gosh, I miss that place.'"

FANELLI'S

NEARLY A DECADE ago, Superstorm Sandy hit New York, and with no power downtown, SoHo was deserted, dark, and cold. But at Fanelli's, there were candles on the bar, plenty of booze, and food for as long as it lasted. Most important, there was company and conversation. "I was here the whole time," says Sasha Noe, owner of the neighborhood café at the corner of Prince and Mercer Streets. "Where else could I be?"

In his fifties, Sasha, an artist and sculptor who can often be found up at six in the morning making repairs, is hanging on with determination. Born a couple of blocks away, he lives with his wife and three kids in the loft where he grew up. His father, Hans Noe, an architect, bought the building where Fanelli's occupied the ground floor in 1982 and ran the bar. Sasha bussed tables and tended bar during high school. After he graduated from Bard, he came back home.

Fanelli's is the second-oldest watering hole in New York. The building went up in 1847. For a while in the nineteenth century, it was a grocery store (when groceries sold alcohol); from 1863 on, it was a saloon.

The vintage neon sign that juts out from the brick building reads FANELLI CAFÉ. The old wooden front door is set with engraved frosted glass. Inside, the bar itself, a long stretch of mahogany, runs almost the length of the room. Clare Huntington, one of the regular bartenders, says, "Fanelli's is one of the last good barrooms left in the city." People blow in from every direction to meet at this corner of SoHo to participate in the lost art of conversation while drinking (some in the same seats for decades).

This is where I eat breakfast nearly every day. "Morning is the sweetest, most local time," Sasha says. In these early hours, Fanelli's might be the bar in a little backwater, the café in a small town where everyone gathers. A few other habitués read the papers, sip coffee or an early cocktail, contemplate bacon and eggs or a plate of fries. An occasional tourist goes for the French toast. One day, a denizen of Fanelli's whose garden had gone wild over the summer offered around bags of gorgeous ripe tomatoes and deep green cucumbers.

On the huge "bar back" (it's the elaborate wooden construction with shelves, mirrors, and carvings that faces you), there is a traditional

carved Green Man, the folkloric figure who has existed for millennia and shows up in both secular and ecclesiastical buildings. (You find him in a lot of English pubs, too. Kingsley Amis wrote a book called *The Green Man* about a pagan monster.) The mirrors and bottles on the shelves catch the early-morning sunshine filtering in through the old windows. Clare sets out bottles of wine and slices lemons. I like being at the bar the best when the TV has an old movie on mute and I can eat my bacon with Errol Flynn or Ronald Colman.

Mike Fanelli (first row, far right), as pictured in a flyer for the artist Chris Wilmarth's March 1971 show at the Paula Cooper Gallery, then located a few doors away.

Lining the opposite wall are tables covered in red-and-white-checked cloths. On the wall itself are vintage photos of boxers—Joe Louis, Rocky Marciano, Kid McCoy, Packey McFarland. In the first part of the twentieth century, boxing was a great urban working-class sport, a way up and out. Michael Fanelli, who bought the place, which had long been a saloon, in 1922, had been a fighter himself.

"My Irish grandpa from the Bronx was a boxer," Clare says. She arrived early, before Fanelli's opened, along with a couple of managers—Naomi, Sheena—to set the tables, put the coffee on, and get ready to serve breakfast.

Regulars cherish the charming young women who run Fanelli's. They know who wants a shot of bourbon at ten when the place opens, who wants a grilled cheese on pita, who craves just black coffee. Most of the staff has been at Fanelli's for six, ten, twenty years. Out-of-towners get advice from them about the city. The staff, both men and women, know how to deal with drunks at night. At lunchtime, they work the crowds, serving barbecued wings, tuna salad, BLTs, cheeseburgers, and chili to tourists, some of them in the back room, where, before you enter, you notice words written in gold on the wooden archway: LADIES AND GENTS SITTING ROOM. This is a holdover from a time when it was considered improper for ladies to sit in the actual barroom. On the wall back here are framed liquor licenses that date to 1877.

The burgers are good, the fish-and-chips superior, the soups excellent. Outside on Mercer Street, Fanelli's maintains a soup stall overseen by the truly lovely Tatjana Asla. "New York feeds me, so I love feeding

it," she says. And she does. Chicken and vegetable soup for the ascetic, Moroccan lamb for the gourmet.

In the late nineteenth century, the area around Fanelli's was a vicious red-light district. Parts of *The Alienist*, Caleb Carr's brilliant historical thriller, were set on Prince Street in this era, when there were seedy taverns, gin mills, and brothels. By the twentieth century, it catered to truck drivers and guys who worked manufacturing and small industry—commercial bakers, warehouse workers, men from nearby gas stations in the part of SoHo known as Gasoline Alley.

Owner Sasha Noe behind the bar.

By the 1970s, SoHo artists began to replace that clientele. The late Lynne Reiser, one of the neighborhood's pioneers, recalled: "Old Man Fanelli couldn't understand what was going on, because all he would ever get were the truckers. He was thinking of closing up, but then all these artists showed up and all these gals." Artists! Women! This small corner of New York spun off its axis.

Fanelli's clientele these days is a cosmopolitan assortment—long-term locals, artists, models, union workers, retired admen, and medical marijuana entrepreneurs, according to Clare Huntington. Very late, around one or two in the morning, workers from the Mercer Hotel and other local restaurants and hotels come by, footsore and thirsty.

There are also some panhandlers, guys selling homemade CDs, artists displaying their work on the street, who are part of local life that casual visitors might not notice or might consider an annoyance. "We

Bartender Colin LaBrie and some regulars at Fanelli's.

look after them," Sasha says. There is always water and coffee and the use of the restroom. When Chris, a regular among this group, pops in, a customer might offer him a cheeseburger. He grins. "Some customers buy me a steak," he says.

"If we don't keep something of New York the way it was, what will our kids have?" Sasha says as he eats an onion ring from my plate (the best fried onions in town are at Fanelli's). "I could probably make a bundle selling this building, but what will that leave my kids?" he asks. "I look at it like an old easy chair that has to be taken care of. I'm from New York, and I'm not going anywhere. I love my parents, and I don't think money is the only thing in life. You think the next generation will look back and say, 'Oh how I miss those mini cupcakes, that eight-dollar ice cream'?" He looks around his bar and adds simply, "I love this place."

RAOUL'S

BEFORE THERE WAS Balthazar or Aquagrill or Lucky Strike—the last two sadly gone now—there was Raoul's. In the early 1970s, there wasn't any place much in SoHo where you could get food late at night, except a couple of bars—Bob and Kenn's Broome Street Bar and Fanelli's (both still going strong), the long-gone Food, and maybe Dave's Luncheonette down on Canal and Broadway.

In 1975, a pair of Alsatian brothers, Serge and Guy Raoul, opened the Prince Street bistro in what had been an old Italian restaurant. They had no real idea if it would even work in an area of town occupied mostly by abandoned buildings, gas stations, and warehouses where rags and paper were stored (and went up in flames on a regular basis). The buildings were scarred with graffiti, and plenty of homeless guys camped out in cardboard boxes. But the artists had arrived, and in their wake, uptown collectors who adored slumming in SoHo and could be seen stepping delicately out of their limos.

Raoul's has been a fixture on this stretch of
Prince Street for forty-five years.

Karim Raoul, the second generation of the Raoul family to own and run the restaurant, sitting at the bar.

The front room at Raoul's.

Back then, it was always a party at Raoul's. They served up steak-frites and great appetizers (especially the poireaux vinaigrette), whole fat artichokes, pâté, and duck (in my memory, at least, there was duck), and plenty of red wine. Rob Jones, the legendary maître d', assigned tables not according to how famous you were, but how friendly. Celebrities were mostly artists and writers and people in drag who danced on the bar. It was a late-night kind of place, with plenty of art and drugs, and Rob putting on his wig and coming down the wrought-iron staircase doing Dusty Springfield. It was also the beginning of the AIDS epidemic. When Rob died in the 1990s, a thousand people attended his memorial. I was there. Somebody recalled Rob saying, "Well, I had to get people through the '80s."

Over the last couple of decades, I was away from New York a lot and didn't go to Raoul's much, but more recently, I noticed little knots of people forming outside just before opening time at 5:30, usually looking faintly desperate. So I stopped by.

The white neon sign still glows in the window as it always did. Inside the narrow space is the long mahogany bar with its mirrors and

LEFT TO RIGHT: Founders Serge and Guy Raoul, and lone waiter Billy Cox, on opening day, December 8, 1975.

Art Deco-ish lights. The black-and-cream booths are at the back; the walls are plastered with photographs and paintings of nudes. Django Reinhardt is on the sound system, providing that certain French je ne sais quoi, and, in the dim light, Raoul's feels held in a suspension of nostalgia; sitting at the bar, I'm drenched in the stuff.

"You take away one picture, and people yell," says Karim Raoul. Karim went to NYU and set out to be a documentary filmmaker. In 2010, though, his father, Serge, had a stroke and Raoul's general manager quit. Karim took over. "I was terrified I'd screw it up," he says. "It was baptism by fire."

He didn't screw it up. But then, restaurants are in Karim's blood. His grandparents ran a brasserie in Alsace. Now in his forties, tall and charming, he lives over Raoul's with his wife and two kids. If he's shrewd enough to understand the potency of the past, he recognizes that a secure future needs subtle changes. The food is better. The oysters are still good; so is the signature steak au poivre, thick as your hand. (You can get the cream-and-Cognac sauce in a bottle to take home now.) But there are crab beignets and soft-shell crabs, too, and on weekends, there is brunch. (In the 1970s, nobody in SoHo was awake in time for brunch.) Families stop at Raoul's for fluffy pancakes with salty toffee sauce and yuzu cocktails, strollers parked outside. Sedate couples drink good wine at seven. Late at night, the models, nine feet tall and seemingly all Brazilian, show up with boyish hedge-fund guys.

About those crowds I'd noticed outside: It seems they were waiting for a Raoul's burger. The chef, David Honeysett, eager to avoid the fancy-burger fray, prepares only twelve each evening. Twelve. Like the Apostles. They're topped with the house au poivre sauce, gooey Saint André cheese, wilted watercress, and cornichons and served with fries and more au poivre sauce to dunk them in. Critics have called the Raoul's burger the best in the world. This has, of course, made it as desirable as, say, a Cronut—but much, much better. Karim Raoul was pretty surprised by it, but an entry in contemporary New York foodie folklore can't be bad for business.

One evening, I ask a young woman sitting at the bar why she's at Raoul's. She says that it's the way she thought of old New York as a kid in Wisconsin. She doesn't care if it's an illusion or not; this is the New York City of her dreams.

Maybe Raoul's isn't quite as louche as it was; maybe there's no longer a Rob to get us through the decade. But as I leave, Chris Session, the manager, a tall man in a red shirt, is taking pictures of a family who are in for supper. Handsome, smiling, he feels like Raoul's.

I walk home after midnight. SoHo's cast-iron buildings, once filthy with grime and graffiti, gleam now under a summer moon like poured cream. And on West Broadway, I can just hear the echo of the chicken man. In the 1970s, he sold large yellow plush chickens from a supermarket cart. I still have one at home, molting on my closet floor. Every year, I think about throwing it away, but it reminds me of all the nights I spent at Raoul's.

THE SWEET SMELL OF CELLULOID

FILM FORUM

O **KAY, SOMETIMES THE** film is digital and doesn't really smell of much except the future, if you want to belabor the point. Does digital have a scent? Is it edible? (I once knew a filmmaker who, when he was very young, ate a bit of celluloid to see what it tasted like, or to ingest it, to let it become part of him.) In any case, for taste, there's the very good coffee at Film Forum, and the maple mocha cake sold in the lobby, which is made just for the theater by Betty Bakery in Brooklyn. In fact, I could happily move in and live in this best of all movie theaters in New York, which celebrated its fiftieth birthday in 2020.

There are four screens in the cozy theater on West Houston Street. The other night, one was showing *Mephisto*, a fantastic film I hadn't seen in around forty years, starring a young and seductive Klaus Maria Brandauer. In another screening room was Alex Gibney's *Citizen K*, a

FILM FORUM

1 A PERFECT CANDIDATE
  "BRILLIANT" - STEWART KLEIN

2 OUT OF THE SEVENTIES

3 HEAVY - HELD OVER!

Film Forum director Karen
Cooper (front) and the rest
of the staff, 1996.

documentary about Mikhail Khodorkovsky, the oligarch; several people in back were arguing in Russian—and laughing.

Piano music drifted out of a third screening room, live music for the 1920 silent film *Within Our Gates*. The music was an original composition by Steve Sterner (he's also a distinguished Yiddish actor). "I'm not a pianist," he has said. "I'm a piano player, a hack." That may be, but he's one of the last of them who can accompany silent movies. Over a period of thirty-five years, he has written scores for hundreds of silent films shown at the Forum. He also often plays for the kids' screenings on Saturdays, when children (of all ages) are invited in to see the silents, as well as greats such as *Some Like It Hot*, *Guys and Dolls*, *Singin' in the Rain*, and *The Wiz*.

Every day, you can see at least four different movies here, old and new, fiction and docs, black-and-white, foreign, American. There are premieres of great indie films like Marco Bellocchio's *The Traitor* and *Christ Stopped at Eboli*, as well as world-shaking documentaries like D. A. Pennebaker's *The War Room* and *Paris Is Burning*, Bruce Weber's *Let's Get Lost*, and Michael Apted's *28 Up* series. There are revivals and festivals—Madcap Manhattan, Manhattan Noir, the films of Kenji Mizoguchi, films by Jean-Pierre Melville and Alfred Hitchcock, events with the great film historian Kevin Brownlow, Egyptian musicals. My favorite pictures—*On the Waterfront*, *The Third Man*, *Kind Hearts and Coronets*—return regularly, often in gorgeous new prints. It goes on and on. Film Forum's famous calendars are attached to fridge doors all over New York.

Once, New York had scores of art houses, revival cinemas, spaces for film festivals—the Thalia, the Bleecker Street, the Carnegie Hall, the Fifth Avenue, the Baronet and Coronet. They are gone now. Park the nostalgia, though; Film Forum is better than all of them.

Fifty premieres of indie films and great new documentaries a year, five to six hundred films all told when you include the revivals and repertory programs, and that good coffee and mocha cake. Film Forum, after more than fifty years, is a miracle.

The old-fashioned marquee—white light, black let-   A postcard from
ters slotted in—lures you in with movies you know and   Film Forum.
love, some you've never heard of, others you had once
admired and almost forgotten, like *Mr. Klein*. Last year, I wanted to see
this Joseph Losey film with Alain Delon, but when I went to the theater,
it was sold out. In the middle of the week, people were lining up around
the block to see a 1976 film in French about an aristocrat who gets caught
in the roundup of Parisian Jews. We are not talking Marvel comics here.

I could stay at Film Forum all day and night. Since its most recent
renovation, in 2018, the theater has become very comfy and agreeable.
"'Love the movies, hate the seats,' had been the basic message over the
years," says Karen Cooper, the Forum's director. In the lobby, they now
sell decent popcorn and ice cream as well as the delicious cake. There
are old movie posters on the walls, videos are shown, and the waiting
audiences are various, funny, self-obsessed, anxious to get the "best"
seats (it's New York), and sometimes delightful in their anticipation; the
friendliest by far, the most eager to see a film of any group I've waited
with, was a group of fans who had come for the opening of *Amazing
Grace*, featuring Aretha Franklin; a few were singing to themselves. The
lobby is a kind of entertainment in itself.

Is all this hyperbole? Maybe, but this little movie house in SoHo is, for me, the ultimate multiplex, one of the great cultural institutions in the city. To be in the New York stratosphere, you gotta be really good. "In brief . . . the best of everything is good enough for me," as Tony Curtis playing Sidney Falco says in *The Sweet Smell of Success*, one of Film Forum's favorite revivals. Bruce Goldstein, who programs all the revivals and festivals, used to give *Sweet Smell of Success* tours of New York. Bruce is one of the most convincingly New York–centric people I've ever met. To paraphrase Mia Farrow in Woody Allen's *Husbands and Wives*, he couldn't survive off the island of Manhattan for more than forty-eight hours.

Another dyed-in-the-wool New Yorker, Karen Cooper never thought she'd be involved with movies. As a girl in Queens, she already had her eye on Manhattan and the arts—as a teenager, she saw Nureyev and Fonteyn dance, watched *West Side Story*, and hung around MoMA. Painting, literature, dance—these were her idea of great culture. When she graduated from Smith and went looking for a job, there was a recession on, and what she was offered was a position running a "teeny little screening room with fifty seats on the Upper West Side." Unfazed, Cooper turned that early version of Film Forum, with its budget of $19,000, into today's four-screen theater on West Houston Street. "I made it up as I went along," says Cooper. She and her colleague Mike Maggiore have programmed all the premieres. They go to festivals, talk to filmmakers. "In the early days, people thought audiences would be put off by the D word," Cooper says about documentaries. A committed activist, she has always been fiercely political, and she has put on movies about Nazis, about the gulags, about the disappeared in Latin America. Of the scores of documentaries Film Forum has screened, one of the most significant, she says, was Spike Lee's *4 Little Girls*, which helped reopen the FBI investigation into the Birmingham church bombing that killed four children and helped galvanize the civil rights movement.

Like all movie theaters, Film Forum was threatened over the years, first by the arrival of the VCR and then by online streaming, but Cooper and Goldstein have learned to stop worrying and love technology.

Instead, what Bruce Goldstein worries about is that controversial movies will no longer be shown. "You have to see what you need to hate."

Goldstein feels it's his duty to make sure everything is seen, and seen in the best possible form. "We're in a golden age of film restoration," he says. He can choose whether to show movies in the original 35mm or in digital 4K, whichever he feels gives viewers the best sense of the movie. He searches everywhere for the best prints and chases them down.

This is a community of people who love movies, who have opinions, who come to laugh and cry, to fight over point of view, to consider how the world looks and where it's going. Karen Cooper predicts that "smart documentaries are the most important films on the horizon," adding, "As a people, we have to get serious about understanding the world around us. Documentaries can help us move in that direction." I love that.

When the end of the world comes, Film Forum might well be the first building I'd help save from the apocalypse—at least I could spend the end times at the movies, in my favorite seat there (halfway down, on the aisle).

WHERE NEW YORKERS SAMPLE
LA DOLCE VITA
———

CAFFÈ DANTE

YOU DON'T NEED to be American to be a real New Yorker. What it takes is a certain love for this improbable, impossible, mythic city when it's really in trouble, damaged, hurting. Australians Linden Pride and Nathalie Hudson always loved New York, so much so that in the aftermath of 9/11, they wished they were here to help out in person. By 2015, they had made their home here in the city and were the owners of Dante, the acclaimed Greenwich Village café and cocktail bar, and just after the 2020 pandemic lockdown was announced, they began sending meals—thousands of them, paid for by Dante and their fans on social media—to hospitals around the city. On some days, they just packed up their car themselves and drove food as far uptown as New York–Presbyterian in Washington Heights. "We live here; we just wanted to help," says Hudson.

The couple, both in their late thirties, are from Sydney. Over the years, they had visited New York often, and eventually they married and settled in the Village.

Photographs from the old days at Caffè Dante.

It was with great good luck, they say, that they managed to buy the old Caffè Dante—a cherished Italian coffeehouse that dates to 1915. Beloved though it was, it needed sprucing up. The old furniture was worn. The paint was peeling. Hudson, who has a background in international law and none in design, got to work. She and Pride installed new pressed-tin ceilings, "as close in pattern to the originals as possible," she says, and they painted the dark green walls cream to brighten the space.

There wasn't much money for decor, so the couple brought pictures and a mirror from their own home. They found a glass-fronted liquor cabinet at an auction, and they hung black-and-white photographs of Caffè Dante in its earlier days, including one of Mario Flotta, the former owner.

In the morning, there is good coffee and croissants or fresh banana bread; for lunch, panini (prosciutto and provolone or veggie). Behind the bar are Cinzano and Campari, small-batch gins and whiskeys, the bottles glistening in the sunlight.

But Dante is most glamorous at cocktail time. The new iteration of the café has made its name on its cocktails, and it serves martinis, Manhattans, Pimm's, and margaritas, often with spiffy variations on these classics. But the heart of the cocktail menu remains Italian: There are Negronis—some laced with strange but delicious flavors such as lavender or chocolate—Aperol spritzes, Americanos, and Garibaldis (Campari with "fluffy" orange juice).

"Around 2015, it became especially trendy to go to the Italian capital," says Melissa Middleberg, a young painter who lives near Dante. "Everybody was crazy about the aperitivo hour."

That Italian thing resonated with Hudson and Pride; many Italians had settled in Sydney after the war (la dolce vita never was limited to Rome, after all). "Caffè Dante reminded us of the old coffeehouses we grew up with," says Pride. "It was the connection to community, the daily rituals that were so important."

Nathalie Hudson and Linden Pride, the
current owners of the café.

Dante's signature cocktail,
the Negroni.

In the back of the café, where Hudson has hung floral wallpaper,
is the kitchen, in which chef Angel Fernandez turns out very good
pastas—spaghetti with fennel and peas, tagliatelle with wild boar ragù—
as well as roast chicken and a fruit-laden apple tart with a flaky crust.
He is also the chef at Dante West, the couple's new seafood joint on the
corner of Hudson and Perry. Everything is cooked in a coal-fired oven,
including the to-die-for bread and the spicy chicken, which is among the
great fowls of Manhattan.

One afternoon, I head over to Dante for a panini and a bicicletta
(Campari, dry sparkling wine, Pellegrino—with its deep pink color and
the orange slice, it looks like a gaudy sunset), hoping to nab the cream-
and-green banquette in the window. These seats, Hudson says, "are
everyone's favorite, and were once reserved for the widows of the Mafia
that used to frequent Dante daily at four p.m."

It can be difficult to unweave Mafia fact and fiction (parts of *The
Godfather* were shot at nearby Caffè Reggio), but Dante's origins are deeply
embedded in the old Italian neighborhood. Between 1900 and 1914, the
largest wave of Italian immigrants—about two million—arrived in New

Al Pacino leaving
Caffè Dante.
York. By 1930, about a million Italians had settled in the city, many of them downtown in an area south of Grand Street that stretched east to Mulberry and Mott Streets, west to Carmine, and north to Washington Square Park. MacDougal Street was one of the main thoroughfares, where many Italian restaurants, shops, and coffee-houses had opened—among them, Caffè Dante.

The earliest of its owners are now forgotten (many of the records were lost during various renovations over the decades), but in 1971, Mario Flotta bought it. It had survived because of its cozy ambiance, because you could sit all day over a single espresso, and because it attracted the writers, artists, musicians, and activists who made Greenwich Village "America's Left Bank," as it was unofficially known then.

As early as the 1910s and through much of the twentieth century, MacDougal was home to people like Emma Goldman, Eugene O'Neill, and Sinclair Lewis, who could often be found at the Liberal Club three blocks north. Hemingway and E. E. Cummings drank at Minetta Tavern, also on MacDougal. In the '60s, Jimi Hendrix played at Cafe Wha? at 115 MacDougal. Bob Dylan lived at number 94.

Former owner Mario Flotta Sr. and his son Mario Flotta Jr. standing with customers outside the cafe, 1970s.

Leni Wolfenson (owner of Smudge Studio on nearby Carmine Street) and his father.

Since the 2000s, much of the neighborhood has been overtaken by sports bars and comedy clubs and joints selling kebabs to NYU students and tourists. But there are still reminders of the old Italian neighborhood. On the same block as Dante is Villa Mosconi, a great red-sauce restaurant where I've been eating for most of my life. Around the corner on West Houston, Raffetto's still sells fresh pasta, as it has for over a century. And across Houston, on Sullivan Street, are St. Anthony's Church and Pino's, the butcher shop (opened in 1904), where along with wonderful beef—I love the Newport steaks—you can get Italian sausage and prosciutto, where there is often opera playing, and where the Cinquemanis, father and sons, call out "Ciao" as you leave.

Customers and staff at Dante seem to have absorbed some of this old Italian gusto and sense of family. "It can be very scene-y on, say, Thursday nights," says Middleberg. "But it's lovely to linger in the afternoon over a cappuccino." And regardless of the crowds, "The people who work at Dante really try to make you feel taken care of right from the first interaction," adds Breanne Sommer, a bartender and former cookbook publicist. "You don't get that kind of attention everywhere in New York."

I'd been passing Dante for decades, sometimes stopping for a quick coffee at one of the streetside tables. When I first saw the new incarnation after Hudson and Pride bought it, I thought, *There goes the neighborhood; another landmark gone. No more espressos, no more memories, no more Signor Flotta to welcome you.* I stamped my foot right into a muddy sludge of sentimentality—and regretted it. Because what has really happened on MacDougal Street is that the new Dante is more stylish, and serves better coffee and food and cocktails.

The sight of a few white subway tiles might have sent some locals into paroxysms of despair, inspiring accusations that the young Australian couple were killing another piece of a disappearing Greenwich Village. But that world was already long gone. Heresy it may be, but if you don't embrace change in New York, you can drown in nostalgia and misery. New York adapts, changes, survives, and that is what makes it the city we love, even as we miss what it once was. There's nothing to do but sit outside at Dante, drink an Aperol spritz, and look back on my life in Greenwich Village.

THREE LIVES & COMPANY

A **WHILE BACK, IT** appeared that Three Lives & Company, the much-loved bookshop in Greenwich Village, had shut. Its customers wept. For nearly fifty years, the little corner shop at Waverly Place and West 10th had remained exactly as it was in the beginning: sweetly bookish, with a literate staff who really like to read. And now it had seemingly gone, and the news traveled down the hotline of despair where there are regular reports that nothing at all is left of the Village to remind you of its bohemian glory days.

Where would I buy books, I wondered. How would I get advice from Nora, who though very young, seems to know exactly what I want? Where would I go to gossip with Troy, to find a translation of *War and Peace* I could finally enjoy, to nag Toby for an advance copy of that new

Le Carré novel? People rent their clothes and beat their breasts and prepared for days—no, for a lifetime—of despair.

News of this end of days was, however, a little exaggerated, as it turned out; the building was merely undergoing structural work. When I went back early on a recent Sunday, NPR was playing softly in the background and the sun was shining through the windows, where new books were displayed on the original wood table and bookshelves. The old glass-shaded library lamps overhead provided good light for browsing. And Toby Cox, who bought Three Lives in 2001, was back behind the desk.

"Bookselling is where I wanted to be, even if I didn't know it at first," he says. Like so many people who love their trade, Toby "backed into the business." He had a job in publishing when his brother, who lived in the Village, "stumbled into Three Lives and became a regular." Toby followed.

Books fill the whole shop—on all the shelves, on the long tables, at the front desk: paperbacks and hardcovers; fiction, history, crime; a terrific section on New York City that includes the first book from the

LEFT TO RIGHT: Booksellers Joyce McNamara, Toby Cox, and Troy Chatterton.

Three Lives Press, *The Last Leaf*, O. Henry's tale of art and life in old Greenwich Village.

As soon as Troy Chatterton, the manager, opens the door, customers rush into Three Lives as if for a fix of singularly restorative oxygen. (I like to think of Three Lives as a secret garden hidden from the city streets.) There is the low chatter of people talking to each other, to friends and strangers alike, discussing books, offering opinions.

"The best kind of customer," says Joyce McNamara, who has worked at Three Lives for twenty years, "is the kind who spends an hour just looking at everything and absorbing it and maybe asks what you think." Joyce actually took the job because of a book. "I saw Michael Cunningham's acknowledgment of Three Lives in *The Hours*, and I was charmed," she says.

It's the staff that animates Three Lives and gives it a particular humanity. "I always ask advice," says Michael Gilsenan, a professor of anthropology at NYU who lives near Washington Square Park and visits

Customers browsing the books with the usual focus,
intensity, and delight found at Three Lives.

This corner has had "three lives" of its own: before the bookshop, it was home to Silbers Pharmacy (which was famously painted by Edward Hopper in 1927) as well as Angelo's Market (pictured here).

the shop at least once a week. "The staff is always engaged by anything you're interested in, ready with suggestions for related writings and to immediately explore available editions with you. It's a truly open place."

"I loved the idea of a corner bookshop," Toby says. "It's part of what the Village means, a welcoming face, a place where people hear about books and neighbors leave their keys."

This is a corner with history. When Edward Hopper painted the building in 1927, it was home to Silbers Pharmacy. Later, when much of the Village was still Italian, it was Angelo's Market. Across the street is Julius', the oldest gay bar in New York, where a 1966 "sip-in" was an early part of the gay rights movement.

On the walls of Three Lives, there is a photograph of Anthony Perkins and Christopher Walken at Julius' when they were filming *Next Stop, Greenwich Village*, and another of Dylan Thomas at the White Horse Tavern—a couple of blocks west—where he more or less drank himself to death. There's a little picture of Gertrude Stein, too, and a snapshot of the three women who started Three Lives in 1978.

Jill Dunbar, Jenny Feder, and Helene Webb opened the shop at a time when, if New York had fallen on hard times, the Village was still its old, somewhat shabby self. It had scores of bookshops, and people inhabited them the way they hang out in Starbucks today. These shops rarely served coffee or food or sold souvenirs, though. What they had were books. Companionship. Ideas. Maybe sex—plenty of people met in bookshops.

"Everyone came to the shop," says Feder. "Our neighborhood had actors, writers, publishing people, artists—almost anyone who was involved in the arts at the time passed through the shop. They helped create it."

All these years later, Three Lives is still jammed on the weekends. So maybe it is true, as Joyce McNamara notes, that bestseller lists rule and customers show up with celebrity book club lists in hand. But people are still buying books. I can remember when you had to take a number to get a copy of the new Haruki Murakami novel going on sale at Three Lives one midnight, resulting in a Harry Potter–style frenzy. There are even a few customers of Three Lives who regularly buy obscure Norwegian novels, or Czech poems in translation.

As one longtime customer says of Three Lives, "The thing I love is that it looks like what a Hollywood set designer thinks a New York bookstore would look like, and acts like one, too." She adds, "There's real thought and curation in the selection: It's the platonic ideal of a New York independent business. The merriness, the energy, the bustle of the place is a sweet reminder that true romance does still exist in New York retail."

So if the book business is necessarily more commercial than in our dreams, well, it is after all alleged that Gertrude Stein herself said, "Whoever said money can't buy happiness didn't know where to shop."

A FEW MORE BOOKSHOPS

When I was growing up in Greenwich Village, the corner bookstore was as fixed a part of the cityscape as the local tavern, and a family stroll after supper always included a visit to one— and an ice cream from Bigelow's drugstore. "I can't tell you how many families brought their kids in after a walk and started them on a lifetime of reading," Jenny Feder, one of the Three Lives' founders, says. What follows is just a partial list of the many lovely shops that keep us New Yorkers in books.

THE DRAMA BOOK SHOP

The Drama Book Shop, where for more than a century after its founding in 1917 you could get theater books and scripts, was about to go out of business in 2019 when it was bought by actor/playwright Lin-Manuel Miranda and some of his *Hamilton* colleagues and relocated to West 39th Street. "When I was in high school," Miranda has said, "I would go to the old location and sit on the floor and read plays—I didn't have the money to buy them. After college, Tommy Kail and I met in the basement, and I wrote a good deal of *In the Heights* there." Alexander Hamilton probably didn't frequent midtown bookstores;

more likely he spent his free time up at the Grange in Hamilton Heights. But he was a reader, and I like to think would have been pleased to have funded a shop like this.

KITCHEN ARTS & LETTERS

Need a cookbook? A first edition of *Mrs Beeton's Book of Household Management*? An apron that belonged to Julia Child? A book signed by Joël Robuchon? Kitchen Arts & Letters, on Lexington Avenue between 93rd and 94th, is the place. With books about wine and herbs, food science, beans, okra, fish, various national cuisines, baking cookies, and more, this shop is the mecca for cooks, gourmets, and those like me who read cookbooks and books on wine in bed, at night, in a kind of gluttonous daze, only to dream about lemon tarts and perfect fried chicken.

THE CORNER BOOKSTORE

This perfect neighborhood shop, on 93rd and Madison, has been selling a beautifully curated assortment of fiction, travel guides, and children's books since 1978.

THE MYSTERIOUS BOOKSHOP

In the world of mysteries, Otto Penzler is the name to know. His bookshop, tucked away on Warren Street, is, for the mystery buff, an astonishing treasure trove. It has hard-boiled detective stories; true crime; thrillers; and espionage, including my own favorites, Ross Macdonald, Walter Mosley, and British greats John le Carré and Ruth Rendell.

ALBERTINE

Like the very elegant brigade of a welcome army, the French now occupy the Payne Whitney Mansion—a Stanford White building opposite the Metropolitan Museum. They have kept up the acres of marble, the winding staircases, the high windows and added even more élan.

Part of the idea for Albertine was rooted in the cafés of Paris—a place where you could read, chat, think, while away an afternoon perusing the latest French titles under a constellation of hand-painted stars.

In an age when translation has been recognized as an art form in its own right, Albertine has not only the best collection of French books in the city, but also that of books translated from the French. Every year, it presents the Albertine Prize to a great translator. Few are more distinguished than my friend Frank Wynne. I asked him about the business of translations. "It is not a matter of finding equivalent words (since there is never an exact equivalence)," Frank said, "but of weighing the weight and heft of words while striving to preserve the cadence and the rhythm of a sentence, to produce a voice that lives on the page. . . . It is impossible to imagine the evolution of the English novel without the availability of translations."

ARGOSY BOOK STORE

One of the prettiest bookshops in town, Argosy has six floors of rare antiquarian volumes, out-of-print books, old maps and prints and autographs, and that certain special hush that comes only from customers who are obsessed with books. Opened in 1925, the shop is now in its third generation of family ownership.

STRAND BOOK STORE

If you want absolutely *everything* in the way of books, head to the Strand, which has been a fixture near Union Square since 1927.

JULIUS'

T'S EARLY EVENING at Julius', the bar on the corner of Waverly Place and West 10th in Greenwich Village where later tonight, the monthly Mattachine Society party will take place, in honor of that gay rights organization founded in 1950.

On one memorable night in 2015, the theme of that event was Oliver Sacks, the great writer and neurologist, who had then recently come out in his wonderful memoir *On the Move*. Sacks showed up at Julius' with his partner (Sacks preferred the term "lover"), Bill Hayes, that night. Hayes later wrote a piece in which he recalled that after he'd introduced Sacks to the bartender, a voice came over the loudspeaker announcing, "Gentlemen? Ladies? Queens? May I have your attention? I have just been told that Dr. Oliver Sacks is in the house—welcome to Oliver Sacks Night, Dr. Sacks!"

There was huge applause, and Sacks was delighted—even more so, according to Hayes, when after he placed his drink order with a tall drag

queen, she squeezed his upper arm and said, "You got it, babe. And by the way, nice biceps."

This is a very Julius' kind of story, it seems to me, because the bar—crowded, loud, and famous as the oldest gay bar in New York, or maybe the country—has a sweet style.

I'm here with my friend Troy Chatterton, who manages the Three Lives bookshop across the street. He is a regular at Julius', and we're sitting in a corner at the front of the room and eating the legendary juicy cheeseburgers from the grill. "I love Julius'," Troy tells me. "I only dip in from time to time, but it never disappoints. No matter what is going on in the world, or in one's personal life, Julius' is open, and a place to always be in good, interesting company, with music, a drink, and a bite to eat (made to order!)."

Already the long narrow bar area and the back room are packed. Photos cover the walls, pictures of people who have frequented the bar, of movie stars, even of a wedding that took place here not long ago. Boxers, too—like every bar in downtown Manhattan, Julius' has its collection of vintage fighters.

A sip-in protest by the Mattachine Society, the early gay rights organization, 1966.

Also on the wall is a photograph from 1966. In it is a group of men, all in dark suits, white shirts, and narrow ties—even the bartender has a tie on—holding the first, now famous sip-in. In those days, it was illegal for gay men to drink in bars, and this event was an early act of protest. Inside the bar, Dick Leitsch had announced politely, "We are homosexuals. We are orderly. We intend to remain orderly, and we are asking for service." The next day, the *New York Times* ran the headline "3 Deviates Invite Exclusion by Bars." More sip-ins followed; they became one of the means by which gay bars were eventually made legal.

There are a few other women here tonight, but mostly it's guys—old and young, in T-shirts and jeans, in jackets and ties, some on their own, some in groups, some with partners or husbands. How astonished and presumably thrilled the guys in that 1966 photo would have been at the idea of a man with a husband; all they had wanted was the right to drink.

But Julius' had a much earlier life. The building dates to 1864. It was a speakeasy during Prohibition, and after that, it became a bar. In 1999, Helen Buford and her husband, Eugene, bought it. He ran the bar while

Helen stayed home. She didn't have much to do with Julius' until Eugene died in 2009 and she decided to take over. "I thought I'd have a go. It was quite an experience," she says.

Born in Greece, Helen grew up in Astoria from the age of six, then moved to the suburbs after she and Eugene married. "I only came into New York about four times a year," she says. When she took over the bar as owner, she had to learn everything, about ordering and deliveries and staff. But soon she understood the significance of Julius'. "Once I understood that," she says, "it became a bigger mission. I wanted to care for it and preserve something important."

"Now this is my living room," she says. "My second home, my extended family." Her son, who is twenty-one and looking forward to medical school, is learning to bartend. Until recently, her mother would come in from Queens with Greek cookies she had made for everyone at the bar.

As a way to keep Julius' going, to keep it alive, to bring new life, Helen tried to entice younger people with monthly Mattachine parties. The word spread.

By ten, the placing is buzzing, and I'm hankering for a second cheeseburger. A group of eight young women has been waiting for an hour. They're out on the town and very cute and giggly, so we give up our table to them. They're excited. This is their first time here.

"Everyone comes," Helen says. "Elderly regulars catch up at the end of the week. New young people come. One night I realized that at the bar, in a row, were two gay men, two gay women, and a straight couple." Helen stops for a moment, then adds, "Even now, I sit here thinking about the little six-year-old girl in Astoria I was and how now I own the oldest gay bar in the country. I never felt I fit in anywhere before; I was a quiet kid. But all this just fits."

THE VILLAGE VANGUARD

THERE ARE GREAT jazz clubs in New York City, which is still the capital of jazz music. On the Upper West Side is the glamorous Dizzy's Club at Lincoln Center; in Midtown, the cool Iridium; and in Greenwich Village, Smalls, which is intimate, and the Blue Note, where big acts often play. I really like Smoke Jazz & Supper Club on the Upper West Side for serious music, and Birdland in Midtown, which was named for Charlie Parker. But closest to my heart is the Village Vanguard. Saxophonist Joshua Redman has said that no matter where you sit, there's no room in the world that sounds as good for jazz as this one in Greenwich Village.

It's Monday night at the Vanguard, and in the pie-shaped little room—banquettes along the walls, tables in the middle, waiters slipping

between them to deliver drinks—the Vanguard Jazz Orchestra is playing "Willow Weep for Me." With four-teen musicians tucked neatly onto the tiny bandstand, and those famous acoustics of a room that holds only 120 customers, the sound is indeed big and very beau-tiful. The bandleaders are Douglas Purviance, Dick Oatts, and Nick Marchione, and the orchestra itself dates to 1965, when it started out as the baby of Thad Jones and Mel Lewis. You can hear music here every night of the year—Kenny Barron, Fred Hersch, Ron Carter, Cécile McLorin Salvant, Brad Mehldau, Marcus Roberts.

Members of the Vanguard Orchestra (originally the Thad Jones/Mel Lewis Jazz Orchestra), which has been performing at the club for five decades.

Earlier that day, as I headed to the club, I'd fallen headlong into a sort of melancholy, a nostalgia for a time when there were dozens of clubs in Greenwich Village where you could eat, listen to music, argue politics and art (or you could just walk around if that was all you could afford); even those who are too young to remember miss it.

After walking down the treacherous set of stairs flanked by red walls, I knock on the inner door, and I'm in. It's magic, to be alone at the Vanguard in the middle of the day with owner Deborah Gordon and Jed

Nina Simone getting ready
to perform backstage at
the Vanguard, 1955.

Eisenman, who runs the club with her. Eisenman arrived in 1981. "It was
an old, special place seeming like it needed a conservator even then," he
says. "My sense of that has only increased as time has passed—that it's
more special, that it's more precious, that there are even fewer places like
it, that it's even more in need of being preserved."

Photos of musicians line the walls. The little club echoes with memories. All the coolest ghosts are here. When Deborah's father, Max
Gordon, opened the Vanguard in 1935, it was a club for poets. When he
hired a young singer named Judy Holliday and her pals Betty Comden
and Adolph Green and their friend Leonard Bernstein, the poets pick-
eted. In the 1930s and '40s, you could hear Ben Webster, Lester Young,
and Sidney Bechet for half a buck. Later there were Gerry Mulligan and
Charles Mingus, Anita O'Day and Stan Getz. Maya Angelou worked
here as a calypso singer. Sonny Rollins recorded *A Night at the Village
Vanguard*, and Bill Evans *Sunday Afternoon at the Village Vanguard*. This
is where Lenny Bruce told his stories (and where scenes for the TV
show *The Marvelous Mrs. Maisel* were shot not so long ago—though, as
Deborah points out, "That was nothing like Lenny.").

"From the day I was born," says Deborah, "the club was like another room in our apartment." Her father was here every night. She hung out at the Vanguard after school, knew all the musicians. When her father died in 1989, her mother—Lorraine Gordon, the Queen of Jazz—took over.

Jed says, "Max wasn't very interested in making a lot of money. He was a reluctant capitalist; that's my memory of him. He enjoyed art and magic and the immediacy of an incredible experience much more. That's what he, in my estimation, got out of the Vanguard. Lorraine was the very same way; that's what they were both about for the most part. They didn't want to be slow or go out of business, but, rather than always being packed, they were much more interested in that indescribable thing that can happen sometimes with live music."

Of all the places that make New York forever cool, that satisfy the deep nostalgia for the way it once was but remain a vibrant part of the present, the Vanguard is at the top of the list. So famous is the club, so often has it been written about, all that's left for me to write is about *my* Vanguard, the club I love, the club where, as high school kids, my friends and I snuck in to hear the greats—Miles Davis, John Coltrane, Bill Evans, Dexter Gordon; where I could pass for eighteen and could pretend I might in another life be Juliette Gréco with Miles in Paris; where I learned to really love the music, although looking back, I'm not sure I didn't love what seemed to be the jazz life and the musicians as much as the music itself. Or maybe I'm just a tiny bit smug when I announce to people that I saw Miles and Coltrane and they gape with envy.

We were Greenwich Village kids; this was our turf, what gave us bragging rights. This is where Charles Mingus once kissed my schoolmate Paul—a story that, though I wasn't there, somehow encapsulates my teenage years at the Vanguard.

Paul recalls how, in the fall of 1961, he and his pal Jeff and a "yet to be girlfriend" got to the Vanguard early, stood next to the bar, and waited for Lenny Bruce to go on. "Suddenly," Paul says, "Charlie Mingus lumbered into the club." After Mingus and Bruce engaged in insulting each other, they started laughing and hugged. Then Bruce headed backstage.

Mingus returned to the bar. Paul doesn't remember many people being at the club, but at the bar sat a stunning woman next to a smallish fellow with, if Paul remembers correctly, "wire-rimmed glasses and a sweet smile."

"Who's your friend?" Mingus asked the woman.

"This is Pierre."

"French?"

"Yes."

"Does he speak English?"

"Only French." Mingus pivoted and addressed the handful of those at the bar who were there early. "Anyone here speak French?"

Paul says, "My command of the language had barely made it out of boot camp, but hey, this was Charlie Mingus, whom I kind of worshipped. So I raised my hand and volunteered."

Mingus put his huge arm around Paul. "I want you to ask Pierre a question. I want you to ask him how you say 'I want to suck your pussy' in French."

"In for a sou, in for a franc," Paul recalls thinking. "I was not about to let Charlie Mingus down or, probably more to the point, incur his wrath."

After an amiable exchange, Paul bellied back up to the bar with his answer. "You're not going to believe this, Charlie, but it's the same in both languages: suck, *sucer*; pussy, *la chatte*, the cat." And with God and our two friends as witnesses, Charlie Mingus took Paul in his arms and kissed him on the cheek.

A FEW BLOCKS EAST

WASHINGTON SQUARE PARK

There are bigger parks in New York—Central Park, Riverside Park, Fort Tryon Park (home to the wonderful Cloisters). There are fancy little greenswards like Gramercy Park, which you need a key to enter and which is really only the equivalent of a private London square. But Washington Square Park is *my* park. The park where I was raised, where I went on swings in the playground that is still there, where I ate Good Humor toasted almond ice cream bars, where I made snow angels in the winter.

NYU students see the park as an extension of their campus. Everyone in the Village walks their dogs there. On the western side, men play chess. In the middle of it all is the fountain where little kids splash. In olden times, when I was one of them, when my best friend and I exchanged homemade cupcakes with bloodred frosting for pastel portraits done by locals flogging their talents in the park, we splashed in that fountain all summer. Around us were folkies with guitars, bongo players, a jazz musician wailing on a sax. Poets declaimed, and political rallies were held. In 1917, six artists, including Marcel Duchamp, got inside the Washington Square Arch and climbed to the top, where they tied red balloons to the parapet, lit a little fire, ate and drank and recited poetry, then fired cap guns and proclaimed the area "The Free and Independent Republic of Greenwich Village."

IL BUCO

ACTOR LIEV SCHREIBER remembers his first night at Il Buco vividly—it was also his first night in his new apartment on Bond Street. "In my haste to buy my first home, I neglected to notice the rumbling of the 6 train under my bedroom," he says. "After a few fitful hours trying to convince myself that it sounded like the ocean, I got out of bed and walked up my new street to the restaurant." There he met Roberto Paris, Il Buco's wine director, who told him how stupid he'd been in buying the apartment, but he had something that might help. "It was a wine from Puglia that almost instantly convinced me that I was in fact much closer to the ocean than I thought," recalls Schreiber. "Once I sat down, he brought me a little plate of the most delicious food I had ever tasted. Four perfectly seared pieces of tuna dressed with the most extraordinary olive oil (also from Puglia), giant white beans, onion, and fresh rosemary." He immediately felt better.

Twenty-five years later, when Schreiber still lived on the block, owner Donna Lennard and her crew from Il Buco celebrated their anniversary. Late one Friday night, they started roasting a pig on the street outside the restaurant. By the next day, it was deeply succulent with just the right crackle, and friends and neighbors settled down to a celebratory meal: porchetta sandwiches with blueberry balsamic mostarda, panzanella, ricotta fritters, beer and wine. The pig roast had become something of a ritual to mark significant occasions at Il Buco, and this was a biggie: a quarter century in the life of a New York restaurant is as long as in a dog's years.

I've been coming to Il Buco almost since the beginning, NoHo being only one tiny hood, a ten-minute walk, away from my own SoHo. We New Yorkers are so tribal, so inclined to stick to the few square blocks that define our own neighborhood and its denizens, that only a place as good as Il Buco would find me crossing Houston year after year.

Bond is one of the oldest, most quintessentially urban, little downtown streets. An archaeological dream, it's where Albert Gallatin, who was Madison's and Jefferson's treasury secretary, lived; so, too, did Dr. Harvey Burdell, a mid-nineteenth-century dentist who was famously stabbed to death by his lover. The original Brooks Brothers was here, and so was Robert Mapplethorpe's loft. Now it's all architectural fabulousness— Jerusalem limestone, acres of marble, Gaudí-esque facades guarded by beady-eyed doormen. But Donna Lennard cooking a pig on the side-walk as if it were her backyard makes you feel that Il Buco is actually an Umbrian farmhouse somehow set down—perhaps blown over like Dorothy's house in *The Wizard of Oz*—among the rackety cobblestones and shiny mega-million-dollar condos.

47 Bond Street is Lennard's domain. She lives with her son in an apartment above the restaurant. In the apartment above hers is Paris, who has managed the wine and much else at Il Buco for a couple of decades. At street level outside the restaurant is a little terrace with a few tables. Inside is the bar where locals settle in for a late lunch.

In the dining room, which seats about sixty, you're tucked away from the city's hurly-burly. Pitchers stuffed with sunflowers are set out on the

Crates containing Il Buco's fresh food and imported delicacies arrive constantly.

Owners Donna Lennard and Alberto Avalle in the mid-1990s, when they opened the restaurant.

long bare-wood communal tables. From the ceiling hang quirky chandeliers that might be merely random twisted wood but are actually works of art. With its old furniture (buffets, hutches) casually set with a few antiques, Il Buco looks and feels exactly as intended—not an easy feat when the intention is a mellow ambiance, that of rustic Italy. This is the Umbria of the imagination, but better.

The artist Chuck Close, who's been coming here since the beginning, says, "Il Buco is, in my opinion, the best Italian restaurant in Manhattan. The cuisine is Umbrian (my favorite area of Italy). I love Umbrian wines as well. Very few restaurants in Italy can match Il Buco."

It's evening as Lennard, a stunning woman in her fifties—tan, blond, slim, stylish—makes her way around the restaurant. She's chatting, schmoozing, laughing with friends; everyone at Il Buco is a friend, a member of the family. "I think of Il Buco as a trading post for culture and ideas and food and conversation," Lennard says. "I like to share this life with other people."

Il Buco has always been adored by artists and fashionistas, uptown money and downtown cool—and just plain locals. You wouldn't mistake the crowd for Italian peasants, but everyone looks as if they're having a good time. There's a kind of joy here; there is pleasure in the ambiance, but also, and primarily, in the food and wine.

A little corner of Umbria in NoHo, Il Buco makes you feel as if you're tucked away in a sweet Italian farmhouse.

A friend and I are sharing; ordering too much, we make greedy inroads into the cacio e pepe (which is like a divine intervention), the fat white anchovies, a gazpacho that is a thrilling pink-orange, the exquisite jamón ibérico. There is spaghetti with mussels, sea beans, chili, and parsley. We divvy up a veal chop, though we could have opted for skirt steak with anchovy butter. Did I leave out the flash-fried zucchini blossoms filled with fresh ricotta? Even with all this, we consume a fair amount of the homemade bread served with a flight of fabulous olive oils.

People sit late into the evening. Wine flows. Sergio Jardim, the sommelier on duty that night, pours with a very liberal hand. As he says, the Sicilian red, a Nerello Mascalese 2016 from Mount Etna, is "mind-blowing." A couple at the next table grow more demonstrative with every passing glass.

For dessert there's the panna cotta, creamy, rich, deep, topped with a swirl of ten-year-old balsamic. I might have also added the crostata di frutta stagionale with candied ginger gelato.

The food is so simple that it's wildly sophisticated, lovely to look at but never vain. "I don't like fussy food or too many ingredients," says Lennard the next day. "The menu is always changing—seasonal, Italian with Spanish roots," she adds. Now that everyone is doing farm-to-table, it seems familiar, but back in the nineties, it was a revelation.

It's a sunny afternoon, and we're sitting on Il Buco's terrace. "Hi, Donna," says a guy passing by on a bike. "Hey, Donna," says Maya Lin, the architect. Lennard loves it all. To her, it's about the neighborhood. "You create a place where people come together, where ideas are exchanged, where community is made," she says. "Let's have some Champagne," she adds, displaying a deliciously girly side.

Donna Lennard grew up in Chappaqua and studied film at Duke and NYU. By the 1980s, she was working at Arqua, a stylish wine bar in

Tribeca where she met Alberto Avalle. The two of them decided that what downtown needed was an antiques shop, so they found a space on Bond Street and invited customers to join them for lunch. It turned out the food was what people wanted, and Il Buco was born. More than two decades later, it has grown into a little empire.

A block north on Great Jones Street on the site of an old lumberyard, there is now Il Buco Alimentari & Vineria, which serves meals all day, breakfast to late supper, and also sells olive oil, sel de mer, homemade

bread, and salume. In the summer, the doors are wide open, so you can pop in for a gelato. Next door is Il Buco Vita, which sells dishes, glasses, linens, antiques, terra-cotta jugs and pitchers. And Lennard has just opened a new place in Ibiza.

Lennard knows the source of every cheese and ingredient; she knows the names of everyone who works for her. Says Roberto Paris, "We were three or four people then, and now we're almost two hundred. But there is the same ferocious commitment. I found not only a career but also a place I could call home."

For all these years, Il Buco has drawn us in, newbies and regulars—and Liev Schreiber, too. Ever since that first visit, he says, "I have been going to Il Buco for something special, something that reminds me that the rumble of the 6 train isn't really a train at all but the distant roll and wash of the Mediterranean. They have never disappointed."

A BLOCK DOWN

JOHN DERIAN

John Derian's original shop, at 6 East Second Street, is what a kind of old-fashioned gift shop would look like if it were brilliantly reimagined, with marvelous collages and writing paper, with tchotchkes and antiques, porcelain table lamps, early-twentieth-century landscapes, blown-glass ornaments (including a hanging bat), trays and teapots, playing cards and pet toys, and fabulous postcards. There are plenty of other seductive graphics that hint at Fornasetti or Terry Gilliam, one of the Monty Python tribe who also did their witty and satirical graphics.

INDOCHINE

AT INDOCHINE ON a cold night in December, Catherine Deneuve, her big fur coat tossed with panache over her shoulders, is in the booth next to mine. "The coat is probably so she can go outside to smoke," says Jean-Marc Houmard, one of the restaurant's three owners. A thin, handsome Swiss guy, he began as a waiter in 1986, a couple of years after the French Vietnamese restaurant opened on Lafayette Street.

Indochine has been around for more than thirty-five years, but it's barely changed in any way that matters. It is still improbably ripe, like a good cheese—or a great French movie star.

Outside near the front door is a tiny orange neon sign—in the early days, there was no sign at all. Inside are potted palms, a bar area filled with rattan chairs and sofas, and wallpaper with big green palm fronds, and you feel as if you are on a Hollywood set for a French colonial house in Vietnam, the movie scripted by Marguerite Duras. In the air is the enticing

Appetizers, including spring rolls and dumplings.

Jean-Marc Houmard, one of the owners of Indochine.

odor of lemongrass and celebrity. Farther back along the right wall are the four big green vinyl booths where I'm trying not to stare at Deneuve, but there's alchemy here, and the movie-star glamour infects me with its spell. "This is our theater," Houmard notes, looking at these tables.

Indochine is the only place I've ever felt famous; it's that je ne sais quoi that lingers like a rare air freshener. In the 1980s, Indochine's heyday, everyone came: Madonna, Warhol, Basquiat, Schnabel, Mick and Bowie, and all the supermodels—and Fran Lebowitz, of course, who still does not share her dumplings, as she points out. Years ago I went regularly with Andrée Putman, the great French interior designer whom I'd interviewed and who became a friend. The most glamorous friend I've ever had, Andrée would arrive for dinner in stilettos and her Saint Laurent tuxedo dress, a slash of blond hair over one eye, the red mouth, and an utter lack of pretension. Cigarettes, steak, and red wine were her habits. She was in her sixties then, I think, and nobody was ever as cool. She was also funny. Dinner at Indochine with Andrée made me feel almost as cool as she was, and as famous; this brief moment of attitude is my historical contribution to the downtown '80s.

"I have never stopped going to Indochine," says the writer Salman Rushdie, who recalls his first visit, when there was "amazingly delicious food, improbably stylish

The Indochine martini, made with pineapple-and-ginger-infused vodka, and garnished with mint.

A collection of Indochine chopsticks for famous customers,
including David Bowie and Naomi Campbell.

TAIWAN
INDO CHINE
Sade
Angela Bassett
Naomi Campbell
5/3/98
Alec Baldwin
UMA THURMAN + ETHAN HAWKE
Jessye Norman

LEFT TO RIGHT: Andy Warhol, Jacqueline Schnabel, Jean-Michel Basquiat, Julian Schnabel, and Kenny Scharf at the opening of Indochine.

guests, and impossibly beautiful waitresses." Rushdie's favorite dishes are the fried spring rolls, spicy chicken breast, crispy battered shrimp, and meaty grilled baby back ribs.

Maybe it's the menu as much as the presence of a star or two that's cranking up my nostalgia; the food is sweet, fried, crunchy, spicy. I'm on my second Indochine martini—citrusy vodka infused with ginger, pineapple, and lime juice. And the seemingly seven-foot-tall waitresses with carved cheekbones who wear their own fabulous clothes are just as ridiculously nice as ever.

Melanie Johl, who has worked at Indochine for decades, says, "The dress code is our own interpretation of what we would wear 'out' at a fabulous party . . . so in true New York style, we wear mostly black. It's fun to 'get dressed up' for work, to put some glam in the mix."

I settled in SoHo around the time Indochine opened in the "adjacent" acronym of NoHo; above it are the crumbling Colonnades, a row of 1832 Greek Revival buildings where Astors and Vanderbilts once lived.

The coveted booths
at Indochine.

The area was desolate and thrilling; there were artists
and drag queens, uptown suits and drug dealers.

Way back then, back in the now seemingly distant
1980s, Keith and Brian McNally, a pair of British brothers, owned the downtown nights; first together at Odeon, and then, after
the brothers split up, Brian when he opened Indochine. Celebs, food,
sex, drugs; even the seating was fodder for the tabloids. Uptown came
down. Limos idled at the curb. Eurotrash rolled in with tons of Euro
cash; artists and musicians, young and bohemian in the '70s, got rich in
the '80s. It was the McNallys who reinvented downtown. (In the '90s,
Keith, having gone to Paris and returned, ruled at Balthazar.) If you went
to Indochine, you could drown in the sweet smell of success.

In 1992, when Brian McNally decided to sell, Houmard and his
partners, Michael Callahan and chef Huy Chi Le, bought Indochine.
Houmard, in New York originally for a law firm internship, had worked
nights at Indochine to pay his rent. It didn't take long for him to discover

that he "hated all the lawyers and loved everyone at the restaurant." Still, he worried. The heat of the '80s was wearing thin; the downtown scene was about art as a tourist attraction. "I didn't know if we'd make it," says Houmard, "but then Calvin Klein had his birthday party here."

Of course, I never really was at all famous, but it was fun to go to Indochine in those days and gawp and pretend. In a way, though, I like it better now. I like going early and taking my niece Justine, explaining to her who Catherine Deneuve is (God help me) and sharing a joke with the waitresses. Like Houmard, a lot of the staff has stayed. As he notes, "The continuity makes the difference, the servers, the menu. People don't come here to try new stuff; they want those spring rolls."

The old downtown is long gone, and people bemoan it, but I always think, yet again, if I can't stand the changes, I should get out of the city.

Lafayette Street may now be fancy coffee shops and billion-dollar condos, but after another martini and that steamed Vietnamese coffee cake, I can stroll home and enjoy the breeze, accompanied by a whisper of past and present pleasure. Or is it just the coriander rub on the ribs, and the pineapple in the martini?

CHISHOLM LARSSON GALLERY

'M IN CHELSEA visiting with Robert Chisholm and Lars Larsson, a couple of old friends who own the best vintage poster shop in town. The walls of the small store are lined with framed posters; there are racks of posters, and in back still more of them—fifty thousand in all. Movie posters, political posters, sports posters, and, of course, those French posters advertising wine and aperitifs and holidays on the Côte d'Azur. Over my desk at home hangs a poster of *Stormy Weather*, a stylized piece of art in black and gray with sky-blue lettering that shows Lena Horne and Cab Calloway, with Fats Waller at the piano. I got it from Chisholm Larsson. Another piece I love, a poster for *The Earrings of Madame de . . .* , is in my bedroom. All it shows is the profile of a woman, an earring, a single gloved hand and, in elegant lettering: Charles Boyer, Danielle Darrieux, Vittorio De Sica, Max Ophüls.

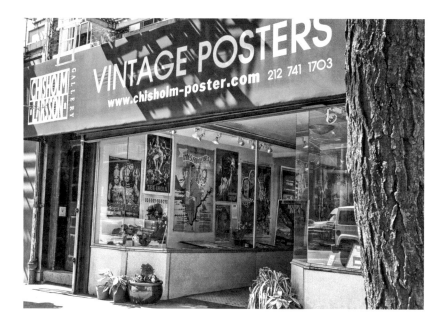

"M&Ms?" asks Lars, offering me the yellow bag. We share an addiction to peanut M&Ms. I'm back to visit but also because a couple of years ago I produced a documentary about Ella Fitzgerald, and I'm desperate to track down the drawing Picasso made of her. The original lithograph is out of my price range, but the poster will be lovely.

Lars and Robert have been selling vintage posters for decades. Their gallery on Eighth Avenue near 17th Street in Chelsea has the old-world cool of a Parisian print shop. The window displays always give the passerby an original angle on the world: classic Swedish films of the twenties, Spanish Civil War propaganda, Egyptian movie musicals, and, my favorite, delectably kitsch Soviet political posters of the 1950s.

The owners are necessarily well informed about price and condition, the whole business of posters. For them (and me), the art and history, and the reasons people want a certain poster, are much more compelling. For instance, as Lars explains, as soon as Communism collapsed in the former Soviet Union, rich Russians, perhaps craving a piece of their history, grabbed them all—sometimes for an ironic taste of the once forbidden, sometimes because the Constructivist movement in the early Soviet years of the 1920s was spectacular. "Right now, the prices for posters featuring

Lars Larsson (left) and
Robert Chisholm, partners
in the gallery.

Soviet space subjects, especially the first man in space, Yuri Gagarin, are skyrocketing!" Lars says. I have my eye on a movie poster titled *Cosmonaut No. 2 in the U.S.A.* It's seven hundred bucks. If I had my choice and a lot of dough, I'd want the original Steinberg Brothers poster for the 1925 film *Battleship Potemkin*, directed by Sergei Eisenstein.

Robert pulls out a Polish film poster for *Nocny Kowboj* (*Midnight Cowboy*). Its blue-black silhouette with a cowboy hat and a pair of large, lewd red lips has mysterious and seedy implications. It's a fine example of the exquisite graphics that have made these pieces by Polish artists so potent and so desirable in the booming vintage-poster market.

Scouring the world for the rarest, most graphically inventive posters, Robert and Lars, along with their protégé, Jason Pellecchia, often hunt down pieces for clients with very specific taste—say, a person looking for *West Side Story* posters in every language. But they also pursue works that catch their own interest: posters from Sweden, posters for films by Italian, French, Chinese, and Hollywood directors.

Part of the thrill is in the hunt. Lars and Robert relish it. I first dropped by the shop years ago looking for a movie poster featuring an unknown American named Dean Reed who became a rock and movie icon in the

USSR and East Germany. "Dean who?" most people asked. Lars just said they'd find one for me. And some time later, he called, and I went in, and there was a poster for a 1970 Italian/Spanish Western titled *Saranda* with Dean Reed in it. Lars had known the exact person to contact in the former East Germany.

A poster for *Le Clan des Gangsters*, a 1970 film with Dean Reed, sometimes known as Comrade Rockstar.

Mention posters, and most people think of cramped souvenir stores with cluttered walls, but Chisholm Larsson presents its stock like a top auction house. The posters are beautifully displayed and cataloged. When you ask for a particular poster, one of the staff will disappear into a back room, then bring out your choice, clip it to a giant artist's board, and leave you to sit, stand, walk around it, and appreciate the graphics to scale (many movie posters are five feet high or more).

The market for vintage posters is constantly on the rise. An "international" version of designer Heinz Schulz-Neudamm's *Metropolis* poster went for $690,000 in a private sale in 2005, making it the most expensive one ever sold. A perfect Dubonnet triptych by A. M. Cassandre, father of the Art Deco poster, has been valued at $200,000.

I'm not in it for the investment. I haven't got that kind of dough anyway. I buy the posters because they are touching and funny and evocative.

Vintage posters serve as a record of sorts, affordable art for people with imagination, style, curiosity, a sense of history—their own and the rest of the world's. The great posters are invested with an entire culture, the way it sees itself, the angle from which it sees others.

An Italian poster for Mel Brooks's original *The Producers* (1967) shows a cartoon of a huge woman, two little men, and the title "Per Favore, Non Toccate le Vecchiette," which translates roughly as "Please Don't Touch the Little Old Ladies." Lars, Robert, Jason, and I spend some time laughing at the old ladies, and then we go out for lunch.

A FEW GOOD SHOPS

In New York City, to shop is to breathe. Many of the grand department stores have gone or are going. I loved them. I grew up in them. My childhood fantasy was to be left alone in Lord & Taylor or Bergdorf Goodman. As for the big-box stores and enormous chains, I'm not sure what place they ever had in my New York. They made things much harder for the mom-and-pop shops and eventually killed off many of them. They gave us a taste for cheap clothes and destroyed any real sense of the value of things.

During the lockdown, many more small shops shut, but others will spring up to take their place; enterprising new people will find something enchanting to sell us. Following is a random and very personal list of little stores around town—and a couple of big but still independent ones—that keep me going and make me happy.

THE FOUNTAIN PEN HOSPITAL

Down near Wall Street is the Fountain Pen Hospital, which has been around since 1946 and can fix anything, including the beat-up, bent gold Montblanc my father somehow acquired long ago. The inks on sale are irresistible; among my favorites are Namiki-Pilot Iroshizuku, a Japanese ink in colors that range from Winter Persimmon to Morning Glory blue, and a gray-blue known as Old Man Winter. Herbin Ink makes ink in Violette Pensée, a shade Oscar Wilde might have chosen.

There are so many exquisite pens, I'd be hard-pressed to choose, but I wouldn't say no to a few in the "back room"; these might include an Aurora Giuseppe Verdi limited edition, a Michel Perchin pen in black enamel and gold vermeil, and the Franz Kafka Montblanc in deep translucent burgundy with silver trim.

JDR

Located on Sullivan Street, JDR sells Il Bisonte, the handsome Florentine leather goods for men and women— bags, briefcases, shoulder bags—that are both tough and refined, as if designed by an Italian who loves the Wild West (*bisonte*, after all, means bison). There are also pieces by French designer Sophie Digard; her one-off originals include wool tote bags featuring three-dimensional flowers made using a technique known as stump work.

DECO JEWELS

On Thompson Street in SoHo is a little shop stuffed with my favorite vintage costume jewelry. Rings with gorgeous paste stones, Bakelite necklaces in wild colors, earrings that dangle and glitter, all from the '30s, '40s, '50s. My recent acquisition of a pair of diamond hoops— each faux stone about two carats—has been admired all over town. The collection of cuff links is astonishing; the vintage Lucite handbags are works of art.

ILANA FINE JEWELRY

Ilana on University Place near Ninth Street opened in 1942, not quite a block from where I grew up. My mother took the family watches and clocks there, and so do I. Repairs aside, Ilana sells a range of unusual silver and turquoise pieces, period watches and jewelry; currently I'm in love with a little diamond butterfly pin.

DE VERA

I know somebody who gave everyone on her Christmas list a glitter-covered rat from De Vera, on West 28th Street. It was a successful season. This is a store with an eccentric collection of jewels, candlesticks, and glass. But you can't beat the jeweled rats for a perfect New York gift.

GRAMERCY TYPEWRITER CO.

If my lovely red Olivetti Valentine ever breaks down, I'll take it to the Gramercy Typewriter Co. on West 17th Street. I covet one of those old Olivetta Lettera machines in the blue case—the typewriter you'd see world-beating reporters use back in prehistory before the computer. There are typewriters that date back as far as the 1930s. And that's the point. The shop is about an almost forgotten time—and one of its biggest fans is a famous collector of vintage typewriters, Tom Hanks. Yes, *that* Tom Hanks. I met Hanks once, and he showed me his collection.

ABC CARPET & HOME

At 888 Broadway is a grand loft building, constructed in 1882 and occupied by ABC Carpet & Home. In an age when the great New York department stores are closing up shop, I'm happy that ABC is very much alive.

The sun glints off the redbrick and cast-iron facade with its carved birds, monsters, and cherubs. Inside, the ground floor gives me a frisson of that age-old infection: the thrill of the bazaar, and the obsessive desire to collect that goes with it. Here's a pink pillow embroidered with dark green trees; there's a fuchsia stone teacup, a vintage crystal chandelier adorned with glass grapes, and an array of deliciously pretty drop earrings. Upstairs are the heaps of astonishing rugs—kilims, dhurries, and Persians so colorful one can almost imagine Scheherazade describing them in one of her stories. And there is the furniture, most of it modern, though at ABC, this still means comfy and runs to fat hot pink velvet swivel chairs and deep leather sofas, and maybe a bergère upholstered in floral satin.

All of this is presided over by Paulette Cole, whose great-grandfather Sam Weinrib, a Jewish immigrant from Austria, peddled used carpet from a pushcart on the Lower East Side. Paulette's father and grandfather opened ABC Carpet in 1947. And in the 1980s, Paulette transformed the company into a home furnishings bazaar that thrills New York to this day.

KEENS STEAKHOUSE

MY FATHER LOVED Keens; so did my uncle Ben. In the New York of the 1950s, for a big night out, you went for steak, and maybe a couple of good martinis. "My father associated prime beef with manhood and having earned enough money for the family to go out and have steak," says Steven Zwerling, a friend and a brilliant New York raconteur. "He planned on eating at every restaurant in Manhattan, but Keens was one of the few places he went back to more than once."

Keens does have stunningly good steak—I think it's the best in New York. With its crunchy black char, the porterhouse for two is a magnificent testament to the carnivorous way of life. And Keens is the only place in town that still serves a mutton chop. It is very meaty and

A staff member fetching a pipe for a gentleman in the Lincoln Room.

The Sixth Avenue Association luncheon at Keens, 1940.

tastes deeply of aged lamb. (It's too aged for me—I actually prefer the double-cut lamb chops, which come from younger lamb and are more tender, and absolutely delicious.)

When Albert Keen opened his restaurant in 1885, in what was then the middle of New York's Theater District, it was called Keens Chophouse. It was a hangout for actors, some of whom would pop in for a chop between acts. The very name "chophouse" suggests a masculine restaurant that serves he-man–style portions. You can almost smell the testosterone. The two main dining rooms are paneled in dark wood. The ceilings are covered with as many as forty-five thousand of the famous churchwarden pipes, the little bowl for tobacco set on a long skinny stem. Each pipe belonged to a particular client; J. P. Morgan, Buffalo Bill Cody, and Albert Einstein all liked a smoke after dinner.

Not only did Keens have a macho reputation as a place where the likes of Teddy Roosevelt, Babe Ruth, and General Douglas MacArthur consumed *meat*, when it first opened, women were completely banned from the restaurant. In 1905, Lillie Langtry, the famous English actress who was King Edward VII's mistress, took Albert Keen to court and

The Clam Bar with the late, much-beloved bartender Edward Hemsley.

won; thereafter, she arrived at the chophouse trailing her feather boa and ate an enormous mutton chop whenever she pleased. A painting of her now hangs above the bar.

After Keen died, the restaurant passed through a series of owners until 1978, when George Schwarz, who had fled Nazi Germany, bought it. It's owned by his estate now and run by longtime manager Bonnie Jenkins. Schwarz invested serious money in renovating Keens, but he kept much of the art, including old prints. Some of these, by Currier and Ives, feature stereotypes of Black people; Schwarz continued to display them as well as some posters for minstrel shows because, Jenkins said, he wanted people to know history—the good and the bad. But in 2019, Jenkins removed some of them. It was time.

You enter the restaurant through a nondescript door on West 36th Street not far from Penn Station and Madison Square Garden—Keens is a favorite place for suburbanites on their way to catch a train home in the evening, or fans after a game. To the right is a large barroom. Everywhere, there are artifacts, grandfather clocks, those pipes, vintage guns. My cousin Johnny (a son of the aforementioned Uncle Ben) describes going into Keens as like falling into an ancient wardrobe full of gear from another age.

This may be a man's world, but it is also somehow very sexy in its own way, dark and secret, tables and booths set in deep corners. When I go to Keens for a late lunch with a long-ago ex-boyfriend, we order cocktails, a Scotch sour for me, bourbon for him. The large menu reads like porn. For starters there are oysters and shrimp, also vast slabs of smoky bacon or a Caesar salad that could feed a platoon of hungry men. The sides are almost as seductive: The spinach is very creamy. The hash browns are crunchy on the outside, soft and mashed within. I love the carrots drowning in butter.

A server in a bow tie brings the porterhouse for two; it could serve four. It is crusty and black outside, and deep red with a tinge of blue within. My friend and I look at it and each other and giggle at the scale; we take a bite and reel with pleasure at the profound meaty taste, that crispy exterior, the almost bloody inside, the excitement of something this *good*. This is like sex with your clothes on, and nobody hurries you to finish.

After a shared slab of key lime pie, we head into the bar for a last drink, Cognac for me, anisette for my pal. Men begin streaming in after work. At the bar is a guy wearing a hat tilted forward, and I imagine him as an underboss in some old-time crime family, like something from a Martin Scorsese movie. I think again of my friend Steven, whose father associated steakhouses not only with manhood but also with an exciting, if slightly dubious, way of life. In the 1950s, Steve's pop owned a bar and grill in Brooklyn, and he admired certain bookies who were not entirely engaged in legal operations. He was taken with what he thought of as a masculine life. For him, Keens represented a particular world, a place of imaginary gangsters and molls, and maybe a few real ones, of men in hats, real men who ate big steaks—a platonic male ideal.

SULLIVAN STREET BAKERY

BACK IN THE mid-1990s, when food as entertainment reached its zenith, when the simple act of buying beautiful comestibles achieved the status of a New York art form, Jim Lahey's loaves were bread celebs. At Lahey's Sullivan Street Bakery in SoHo, people got in line early for the Pugliese oval loaf with its dark-honey-colored crust; the sourdough Pullman; the ciabatta, thin, with a light golden crust; the white pizza. You could smell the bread from a block away.

In the SoHo of yesteryear, there were still artists, crafty types doing artisanal things in lofts, buying groceries at Dean & DeLuca and bread at Sullivan Street. When Lahey moved the bakery, people wept. It wasn't only the bread; it was another sign that the neighborhood was going.

Lahey now bakes his bread on a rackety stretch of the West Side, in a large squat loft building on West 47th Street. The ovens are in back, a

You could call owner Jim Lahey
a bit of a bread subversive, a
baker with a cause.

café in front; Lahey lives upstairs. The whole area, the street, the buildings are among the last vestiges of an industrial city. There are manufacturing buildings and potters' studios. On a weekday morning with
almost nobody around, it reminds me of SoHo when I first moved there.

At a table in the little café, a couple is nibbling on some freshly baked
rolls, sampling the focaccia with rosemary, eyeing the pizza. Like drunks
at a favorite bar, they are giddy. "We come to town for your bread," says
the woman, who notes that they are from San Francisco and that this is
always their first stop in New York.

Lahey comes into the café and chats with them, discussing bread. He
is devout in its pursuit; this is his religion. He appears easygoing; he could
be an old hippie. But inside, there is an original and obsessive baker who
knows what he wants and for whom his trade is all-consuming.

Lahey's shop in Chelsea offers up all his breads, pizzas, pies, and pastries, and the customers come in salivating for more.

I accept a square of pizza. It has a faintly sweet flavor and a slightly crisp crust. The bread baked on West 47th Street is also sold at the café in Chelsea, which serves breakfast—soft-cooked eggs with crispy pancetta on brioche is a favorite—and lunch. I love the sandwiches, best of all the roast beef with oven-roasted tomato, arugula, and aioli on strecci, a foot-long flat baguette made out of pizza dough. There's a ricotta and tomato tartine, or the Cavolfiore pizza with cauliflower, Parmesan, green olives, chili flakes, bread crumbs, and parsley. The range of Italian breads Lahey bakes is almost as great as in the mother country; as often as not, this bread is as good and—heretical as it may be to say—better.

Food writer Ruth Reichl calls Sullivan Street Bakery "the church of bread," but Jim Lahey never envisioned such a life of devotion for himself. As a young guy on Long Island, Lahey dreamed of life as an expat in Italy, where he would work as a sculptor. This notion of living in Europe, of the expat experience, has always held a certain glamour for young Americans; I went to Paris after college to write a novel on a napkin at the café Les Deux Magots, assuming I would run into Simone de Beauvoir. I did. I saw her with Jean-Paul Sartre, who was eating a large ice cream sundae.

In Italy, Lahey discovered bread. (Typical of the best is that from Il Fornaio in Rome's Campo de' Fiori market.) The flavors of the bread, the texture, the way it is an essential part of Italian life seemed as interesting to him as his art; it *was* an art. By the time he came back to New York, Lahey was devoting all his spare time to bread.

"I wanted to bake bread," Lahey says. "This was around 1992, and I baked in a jerry-rigged GE stove in Williamsburg. I was baking bread at night, sometimes all night, and I was running out of steam." Then Joe Allen, founder of the eponymous Theater District restaurant and Lahey's mentor, staked him for a return trip to Italy so he could check out the breads he admired. He talked to bakers, looked at their ovens, sampled what they produced. Fell in love.

Hard to recall that great bread was rare in New York before the 1990s. Even packaged rye bread was considered exotic—an idea that spawned the great ad campaign "You don't have to be Jewish to love Levy's real Jewish rye." True, you could find good bread—bagels, "corn" rye, and, with some difficulty, pita and naan. But you had to look hard; you had to make your way to Little Italy, the Lower East Side, or Atlantic Avenue in Brooklyn. In 1994, with Joe Allen's help, Jim Lahey opened Sullivan Street Bakery, and the stampede was on.

First came locals, the denizens of SoHo who ran to Sullivan Street early not just for the bread but also the biscotti and cornetti, those little Italian croissants, as well as the olive oil cake. News spread. Restaurateurs got wind of the bakery, and soon Lahey was producing bread for them. Real fame came with Lahey's first book, *My Bread*, with its "no knead" method that allowed home bakers to produce high-quality loaves in their own ovens. There followed two more books, *My Pizza*, for which he won considerable kudos, and *The Sullivan Street Bakery Cookbook*.

During the pandemic lockdown in 2020, I thought quite a bit about Lahey and his bread. Everyone seemed to be making bread at home, and there was a run on flour. I thought about baking for around five seconds, and then I called Sullivan Street Bakery and got a brioche loaf, half a dozen pains au chocolat, and some pizza delivered.

Bread is the staff of life, they say. During those long nights of lockdown, I sat at my window, eating the bread with some butter, watching the world go by.

OUR OWN PRIVATE BERNARDIN

LE BERNARDIN

I **WANT MORE OF** those langoustines." This is my cousin Caite, and we're just finishing lunch at Le Bernardin. It is the best restaurant in New York, possibly the world; the French La Liste has consistently rated it in the top slot or at number two since it opened in 1986. And who knows better than the French?

The langoustines were sublime, warm and lightly cooked in a dashi broth, not so much poured as gently drizzled into the bowls, with exquisite finesse, from a little jug by one of the endlessly attentive staff.

Caite and I have come into the restaurant on a grimy, dank winter's day, escaping from 51st Street, in the middle of the busiest part of the city, where the traffic is crazy and the noise cacophonous—trucks honking, people yelling, office workers dripping hot sauce onto tacos from food trucks. Inside Le Bernardin is a different world. The French have a word for it: *dépaysement*. It means, literally, "out of the country," but the real sense of it means to be away, in another world, free of the quotidian.

Éric Ripert and Maguy
Le Coze, partners in Le
Bernardin, at its beginning.

Almost as soon as we are seated, a bowl of salmon rillettes and glasses of La Caravelle arrive at our table. As we sip our Champagne, waiters dance around, bringing the tray of bread—baby baguettes, dense dark pumpernickel slices, fennel and tomato rolls, walnut and raisin bread, all seemingly just out of the oven. The butter is soft and sweet, and when we help ourselves and our knives leave a tiny mark on the surface, the pot of butter is replaced with another one, the surface smooth; no dented butter for us, not at Le Bernardin.

This is dining on a grand scale. It belongs to the timeless New York of the dazzling skyline and the dry martini, the mythic city of the spectacular, of George Gershwin and Duke Ellington, of Jackie Kennedy, of Fred Astaire dancing in the dark in Central Park, of *Hamilton* on Broadway. The glorious dining room is outfitted with orchids in glass holders and lavishly comfortable tables and chairs, a plush carpet, an immense painting of the sea, and exquisite service. Le Bernardin is elegant—palatial, even—but never pompous or grandiose or intimidating. Sleek, stylish, swanky, sexy, it all works because the food and wine are, simply put,

Banana s'more: warm chocolate cake with caramelized banana, smoked meringue, and coquito sauce.

beautiful—but without that "touch me not" quality. This is food to relish, to savor.

My most profoundly cosmopolitan friend, the journalist Vladimir Pozner, who is all at once Russian, French, and American, who has been everywhere and is a real connoisseur of food and wine, tells me, "Le Bernardin . . . say it slowly, say it again, savor it, let it roll off the tip of your tongue. For my money, this is the best restaurant in New York: The service is impeccable, the atmosphere breathes class, and the food is simple and therefore unbelievably difficult to master. It is always perfect, bursting with flavor."

Le Bernardin's roots are in Paris, where, in 1972, Gilbert Le Coze and his sister, Maguy Le Coze, started a restaurant called Les Moines de St. Bernardin. In 1986, soon after they got a third Michelin star in Paris, they moved to New York and opened Le Bernardin. Just eight years later, when he was only forty-nine, Gilbert Le Coze suddenly died of a heart attack. Éric Ripert, who already worked at the restaurant, replaced Gilbert as chef and has worked with Maguy ever since.

As Caite and I have our lunch, Ripert passes through the dining room, greeting guests. He is charming, handsome, blue-eyed, perfectly French, and quite tall, but not at all intimidating. I met with him once in Le Bernardin's kitchen when I was writing a book about Balthazar, the downtown brasserie, and we sat drinking Coke Zero and talking about food. A pal of the late Anthony Bourdain's, Ripert has often been on television, and he is exactly the right French chef for Americans because he is startlingly unpretentious. (Ripert told me that, left to himself, he'd eat simple brasserie food every night, perhaps steak-frites.)

The lack of pomposity makes Le Bernardin a true New York restaurant of the best kind. There is no headwaiter looking you up and down when you arrive. There is never a sense that other guests are treated better than you. And, of course, the food is wonderful, and there's a staggering wine list.

When I was a kid and my parents were going out to dinner big-time, that meant eating French. And not just at a bistro in the Theater District (all of which seemed to be called Pierre au Tunnel or something like it) or a joint in the Village with maybe coq au vin and a smoky candle on the table. For my parents, to celebrate was to go to Le Chambertin, La Caravelle, La Grenouille, La Côte Basque, or, the most revered of all in its day, Le Pavillon. When my mother and father went out on the town, they dressed up, she in her black chiffon dress and satin pumps from Delman. The maître d' at Le Pavillon must have figured my ma was somebody, a star, a society babe, because he treated her beautifully. She basked in it all.

That's how I feel going to Le Bernardin. By the time Caite and I have finished the rillettes and moved on to those langoustines, we are not just eating but sighing.

The staff is formal, impeccable, but also warm and charming, a very hard act to accomplish. The more we eat and sigh and laugh, the happier they all seem, and there are plenty of them, waiters and managers and sommeliers. There is something luxurious about the fact that as soon as you've used your crisp white linen napkin once, it's whisked away and replaced.

Of the dishes, most of which are seafood, my favorite is the scallops, sheer and sumptuous as silk in a ginger and lemongrass broth. And the sautéed sepia "ribbons," cuttlefish with a saffron mussel broth. Then there is barely cooked Faroe Islands salmon; a seductive pink orange, this is salmon from another planet, as sensuous a dish as I've ever had.

We've had two glasses of Champagne, and now the handsome young sommelier in black with his silver tastevin (tasting cup) suggests a glass of white Burgundy. We've passed hour two. Bring on the Burgundy.

And then comes dessert. For Caite, there is a hazelnut sphere covered in real gold leaf, with Frangelico mousse and praline ice cream. For me, a sort of Mont Blanc made of a chestnut crémeux. Also, a pear sorbet nestled in a perfect meringue shell. And finally, a waiter brings what seems to be a pale brown eggshell with its top removed. "Put your spoon in, but don't mix it; just dig down into the layers and eat it," he cautions. Following his advice, we spoon up milk chocolate pot de crème, caramel foam, maple syrup. "What do you call this?" I ask Ripert. "What does it look like?" he asks with only the faintest French amusement.

"An egg?"

"We call it the egg," he replies.

And so, on to the espresso and the mignardises, the little sweets to go with it—a pear pâte de fruits, a coconut macaroon, something blissful in chocolate.

After three hours, Caite and I tumble laughing into the street as if we were in a 1930s comedy about the New York high life.

"You think, *I'm here? Me? Oh my God.*" This is my cousin as we leave Le Bernardin. "This is a *wow* restaurant, this is something, this is . . . ," she adds with a French flourish, ". . . *sensationnel.*"

The main dining room at
Le Bernardin.

SERENDIPITY 3

T'S LATE MORNING on a dank, freezing Saturday just around Christmas, a flurry of snow falling into dirty patches on East 60th Street, but in spite of it, down these mean streets the little children hurry. Run, little kiddies! Run!! Toward the East River, beyond Bloomie's, whose matronly shape takes up an entire square block!!! Past the antique shops, glittering with glass and Art Deco's sharp(!) edges, and some beauty salons. And then there you are!!! To join the anxious parents and little children waiting—if you weren't a New Yorker, you'd think, *What the hell???*—at the kandy-kolored tangerine-flake electric Kool-Aid ice cream parlor.

It is an ice cream parlor that looks like a *weirrrdd* antiques shop, with knickknacks and bibelots and *stuff* on all the shelves and hanging from the ceiling. Some of the memorabilia is legendary: the operating-room lamp, the red chair that was the first seat at Serendipity in 1954,

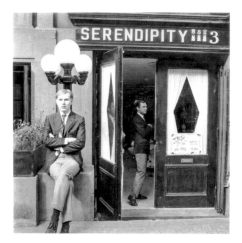

Andy Warhol outside
Serendipity 3, 1962.

the French paintings, and the statue of Andy Warhol, a frequent guest, hanging in the back over his favorite chair. Some say Andy's spirit is living right here.

This is a place where generations of tiny tykes and teeny tots, not to mention large ladies, have clamped their wet, eager mouths around straws and sucked up sink-size bowls of frrrozen (Serendipity's spelling) hot chocolate topped, as Joe, the lovely guy who runs things, says, with "mountains and mountains [ain't no mountain high enough!!!] of whipped cream."

In fact, Serendipity was, in the first place, supposed to be an antiques shop with a little café in the back. In 1954, a trio of young guys, Stephen Bruce, Calvin Holt, and Preston "Patch" Caradine, set it up in this backwater near the river, at a time when its neighbor Bloomingdale's was a local store where you went for sheets and towels and homewares, long before it became the fancy "Bloomie's" of designer lore. Stephen Bruce was a window dresser and a wannabe designer, and it was his taste that influenced the look of the place. He had a knack for searching out the best tchotchkes. This was the age of midcentury designers, sleek and Scandinavian, and people were throwing out a lot of stuff, including Tiffany lamps. (I knew a woman who was given one as a wedding present and got rid of it

The eclectic decor at Serendipity 3 includes a giant old clock rescued from a building on Third Avenue that was being demolished in the late '50s.

because she thought it was old-fashioned.) The owners of Serendipity hung up those lamps, which, as somebody has said, gave the place a psychedelic look, all those colors spinning round on the tables. They put up lampshades with fringes. They piled gewgaws—figurines, dolls, pottery—on shelves right to the ceiling. Holt and Caradine were originally from Arkansas, and they came with a certain Southern charm, as well as recipes for rich pies from their mamas. They installed one of those enormous fancy espresso machines from Little Italy with buttons and levers and wheels. Soon the café became the main point of a trip to Serendipity.

The shop still sells tchotchkes, some vintage, some new, but the early sweets and coffee grew into a full-blown menu, including foot-long hot dogs and chili and variations of the famous frozen drinks.

With the arrival of irresistible items, especially the frozen hot chocolate, came Marilyn Monroe. And Andy Warhol. Later, Cher, and then Oprah, who put it on her bucket list (which I assume is a bucketful of the hot chocolate). Over these past six decades or so, Serendipity has sold twenty-five million frozen chocolate drinks in half a dozen flavors, from Oreo to peanut butter, each in a sort of glass cocktail bowl big enough to bathe a baby in. The last time I took a posse of little children here, a set of delicious twins, Lucy and Harry, locked their lips around the straws, began to suck up the magic bowl of chocolate, and refused to look up until it was drained. *Slurp, slurp!!! Suck!!!* (If you suffer from misophonia, you should not come here.)

Knocking back frozen hot chocolate at Serendipity is a New York ritual, like getting drunk for the first time at the Carlyle. For more than sixty-five years, children have been coming to this place that is like something out of a Tom Wolfe novel because it is so crammed with shiny things that make little kiddies high on sugar *scream*!!! "Boo-hoo, Mommy, boo-hooo–hooo."

The desserts, like the children themselves, are, powie, wowie, the exclamation marks and asterisks of the great bard of New York in its heyday. Like the hippies boarding the kandy-kolored bus in 1963, the kids of New York now run into Serendipity in pursuit of their own mind-altering substances.

Many adults can be seen here, too, of course, sometimes sharing, sometimes not, consuming these wicked, wicked items. Me, I'm waiting for somebody to treat me to the thousand-dollar sundae, which consists of three scoops of Tahitian vanilla ice cream covered with 23 karat gold leaf, almonds, caviar, and a "sugar-forged orchid" that takes eight hours to build, all served in a $350 Baccarat crystal goblet with an 18 karat gold spoon on the side. Can I keep the spoon?

That frrrozen hot chocolate is made with fourteen difference cocoas and milk and ice blended together, then topped with those Everests of whipped cream. But it's not just this one drink that is of a size for giants or giant-killers; everything here is larger than life. The hot dogs are a foot long, the pancakes are "bigger than your head." There are frozen Snickers and frozen Twinkie sundaes, and every kind of fried thing— it's like the food at those state fairs in the Midwest where everything is deep-fried, but on Manhattan's Upper East Side. It's all enough to induce a coma in a child before the sweet stuff rips them out of it and gives them a sugar high. Yum! *Slurp!!* Bingo!!! Bravo!!! Golly!!!! Eureka!!!! Zut alors!!!!

DONOHUE'S STEAK HOUSE

WHEN I THINK of Donohue's, it's like coming home," says Maureen Donohue-Peters, a handsome blue-eyed woman whose grandfather came from Galway, Ireland, and opened this bar and grill on the Upper East Side on March 20, 1950. She recalls the date so specifically because it is important to family legend. Maureen's pop bought out his father soon after, and she joined him in 1980. And, she says, "I never looked back. We're in the third and fourth generation now, this being myself and my two nieces. Crazy as it seems, I still feel my father's presence. This is like an extension of my home, and when people walk in, I want to make them feel like family." Maureen pauses, glances at the evening crowd as it starts arriving, adds, "I treat everyone the same. You don't have to be rich or famous; you just have to be nice. You do what you love, and it's never a day's work."

A few drinkers are already at the bar in the late afternoon. They appear to be retirees of a certain age who pass their time here, a bittersweet scene on a cold, wet day. Maureen knows them all by name, their kids and grandkids, too, and in most cases, their preferred tipple. Donohue's calls itself a steakhouse, but to me, it is a great Irish pub. I get a waft of other times when I duck in off Lexington Avenue between 64th and 65th. This is the lower end of the Upper East Side. It has the settled, comfy feel of prosperous middle age. It makes no difference that realtors have affixed the tag UES to the neighborhood. There is no point to it at all except to jack up prices, to try to make a delightfully staid and old-fashioned area hipper. Trendier. Brand it as cool. Donohue's gives the lie to it. This is an institution where the clientele is well aged and the food is what they might have eaten at prep school. There's meatloaf and Yankee pot roast; there's liver and onions and other vintage eats that include an immense (and delicious) slab of prime rib on Fridays. No kale is served, no tower of seafood, no uni.

Along with the regulars at the bar, you find a few couples in back in the black booths draped in red linen. Two ladies share a club sandwich; each has a couple of Manhattans. I'm in another of those booths for supper with my pal Dubi Leshem, who lives across the street and is a frequent visitor. "It's unpretentious, welcoming, relatively quiet, and a great place for conversation," he says, contemplating his cheeseburger.

Maureen comes by to say hello. She and Dubi are old friends now, and they exchange a little gossip. Dubi says, "Somehow you feel this place will always be here." If it were to shut down, it would be like a death for its regulars, who have always included politicians, journalists, big names in show business—Nelson Rockefeller, Henry Kissinger, Liz Smith, Gay Talese, Jimmy Fallon, and "Billy" Murray, as Maureen calls him. The clientele is loyal. Robert Ellsworth, the late antiques dealer, made the news when he left each of two waitresses at Donohue's fifty grand in his will.

To some extent, this area around Lexington Avenue still feels a little like it did when I was a kid. Near Donohue's are hairdressers, cafés, tea shops, drugstores, dry cleaners, even a few stores selling buttons or

Michael Donohue behind the bar on his first day as its owner, 1950.

wrapping paper. On Lex itself, there's the pet shop full of puppies. And dominating all of it is Bloomingdale's, the grand old lady of Lexington Avenue. This is the old, sweet Upper East Side, with its majestic apartment buildings on Park and Fifth, the more modest apartment houses on Lex, and the brownstones on side streets. In spite of the slick towers on Third Avenue, the overpriced Italian restaurants where hedge-fund types wear pink pants at night in the summer and the women a new face annually, the area remains, for now, a cozy place.

Donohue's has the kind of patina that comes with generations— not patina in the designer sense, but the emotional luster that is produced by seventy years of staff attention and customer affection. Once, there was an Irish pub, a steakhouse and bar, a bar and grill, on

almost every corner in New York City, each with its own clientele and its own style, but most are gone. P.J. Clarke's remains, of course; so do Fanelli's, the Ear Inn, Pete's Tavern, Old Town Bar, McSorley's Old Ale House. Donohue's, too.

As it gets later, the older patrons begin to drift out into the night, the hard-core drinkers guard their seats at the bar, and a younger crowd arrives, many of them the children or grandchildren of Donohue's clients. Says Maureen, "We have customers that have been coming here for fifty years, families for three generations."

The noise grows. The crowd is more raucous. The melancholy disappears, and the present snaps back into place. People eye the back, hoping for a seat—it's first come, first served, and you'd have to be JFK for Maureen to make an exception.

By nine, she is getting ready to go home, leaving her nieces in charge. I'm still working on the prime rib—the meat is very rare and juicy and bigger than the plate. Dubi's cheeseburger is quite tall with a flat top (like an old-fashioned haircut). He says, "I love this menu; it's never changed much. The service is always welcoming, and nobody minds anybody's business." That may be; people keep to themselves, and it would be bad manners to stare at a famous face. But when Maureen heads for the door, every customer looks up and bids her a good night.

THE PARK AVENUE ARMORY

A few blocks up Lex is the Park Avenue Armory, built by New York State's prestigious National Guard Seventh Regiment, the first volunteer militia to respond to President Lincoln's call for troops in 1861. Members of what was known as the "Silk Stocking" regiment came from some of New York's most prominent Gilded Age families, including the Vanderbilts, Van Rensselaers, Roosevelts, Stewarts, Livingstons, and Harrimans.

The armory is enormous, a kind of overwhelming presence, a building where a whole regiment could train. Built as both a military facility and a social club, it has reception rooms on the first floor and company rooms on the second; many were designed and decorated by the likes of Louis Comfort Tiffany, Stanford White, Herter Brothers, and Pottier & Stymus. The armory's 55,000-square-foot drill hall, reminiscent of the original Grand Central Depot and the great train sheds of Europe, is now a theater space, recital hall, and exhibition center.

The scale of the interior allows productions to spread out. I once saw a *Macbeth* in which the whole place was transformed into a dark and murky Scotland, with the audience assigned to different clans; Kenneth Branagh in the title role fought deep in the mud—was it real mud? Stage mud? I couldn't tell. It was theater, after all, and as the player soldiers marched, so seemingly did the ghosts of those who had drilled here long ago.

BEMELMANS BAR

AT **BEMELMANS BAR** in the Carlyle Hotel, a little girl in a red dress with a white lace collar stands by the grand piano and, with some insouciance, as if at six she were auditioning for Broadway, belts out a song from *Annie*. It's a snowy Saturday afternoon in December, Christmastime in the city, and Madeline's tea party is in full swing.

Madeline, of course, is the heroine of the children's book series by Ludwig Bemelmans. As each of the six stories, published between 1939 and 1961, begins: "In an old house in Paris, that was covered with vines, lived twelve little girls in two straight lines. . . . The smallest one was Madeline." And here she is, in her blue coat and big white hat on the wall at the far side of the bar, along with her gang of fellow French school-girls. Famous for the books, Bemelmans was sought out by the hotel to paint the walls of a new bar, opening in 1947, that would be named for him—in exchange for room and board for him and his family for eighteen months. (Not a bad deal.)

As a fat, nosy, inquisitive child, I loved grand hotels, which always seemed to me like fabulous dollhouses, except you could go inside and live in them. They were, I imagined, places where you could slide down the banisters; chat with the uniformed elevator men, who always knew the best gossip; and access that magic number called room service. Of these grand dames, the Carlyle Hotel, on 76th and Madison, is the last. The Plaza as the hotel it used to be is kaput, and who knows what comes next for it? The Waldorf is now mostly apartments. There are scores of great hotels in the city, but none that have the Carlyle's romance.

Conceived in part as a residential hotel, the Carlyle opened in 1930, the same year as the Chrysler Building. It was a very good era for style. Art Deco was the rage. The hotel was farther uptown than most other grand hotels and just a block east of Central Park, where sheep were still allowed to graze (they kept the lawns tidy). But 1930 was also the first full and desperate year of the Great Depression, when a third of New York was out of work and there were shantytowns in the park known as Hoovervilles, where the homeless lived.

Even as the East Side has changed and is now replete with look-alike restaurants and fancy bars, the Carlyle has remained itself: elegant, friendly, discreet. JFK and Marilyn Monroe stayed here at the same time in the early 1960s, the young British royals still do, and Roger Federer has a suite named for him.

The hotel is old but never dusty. During the Met Gala each May, the Carlyle is where everyone changes, and you can stand gawking on the sidewalk as Beyoncé and Cardi B and Billy Porter emerge, exploding from the hotel in wild outfits. The walls not devoted to Madeline are painted with Bemelmans's take on Central Park across the four seasons, which is whimsical and charming with a tiny spritz of irony—like the vermouth in your gin. It's a gloss on the uptown social scene: Here are the animals as they gambol on the green, the indolent elephant with a parasol, the raffish bunny in a boater, the giraffe family, the father tipping his bowler hat to the mother.

Me, my niece Justine, and her daughter, Rosie, at a Madeline tea party.

A Madeline doll perched in front of a mural depicting a scene from the classic children's story.

At the Madeline tea party, the little girl in the red dress has finished singing and is plundering the buffet table for cupcakes and miniature burgers and frosted cookies in the shape of the Eiffel Tower. On the chocolate leather banquettes lining the walls sit the daddies and mummies and grannies, eyeing—a little wistfully—a few adult interlopers who are drinking cocktails at the bar. At the grand piano is Tina deVaron, a terrific musician and a genius child wrangler, and she has the kids singing and dancing, calling out favorites; even the chubby two-year-old in blue is boogying with style. "Raindrops on roses and whiskers on kittens . . ." (Now I can't get it out of my head!) And on the bar and tables and piano are piles of Madeline dolls and books, as well as embroidered napkins and painted plates in honor of the little girl who was born in 1939.

All of this leaves me swamped by terrible, seasonable nostalgia for my own childhood Christmases in New York, which included the miraculous windows at Lord & Taylor, greedy visits to FAO Schwarz, making snow angels in Washington Square Park, seeing the Rockettes at Radio City Music Hall, and skating in Central Park (watch me spin!), followed by hot chocolate at the Carlyle, with plenty of whipped cream.

Bemelmans's wall mural of well-dressed
animals in Central Park.

Before too long, the children at Madeline's tea party today will be back at Bemelmans Bar, this time with a white-coated waiter delivering their martinis in frosted carafes to the nickel-trimmed black glass tables.

Tina deVaron entertaining the kiddies at a Madeline tea party.

At around five this evening, the cocktail crowd filters in, first older local couples in suits and dresses and pearls, later young people, some in preppy plaid pants and blazers. Tourists cram in, too. There is a youthful military man in a red dress uniform with medals and ribbons hanging from it like ornaments on a Christmas tree.

Frank Bowling, who was the general manager of the Carlyle in the '80s, says, "To me, Bemelmans was like a Whit Stillman movie, all Upper East Side but also comfy. I'd stand at the side and watch the phenomenon. I remember one night when Tony Bennett just got up and sang. As fancy as it is, it's a real neighborhood bar."

In the evenings, the composer and musician Earl Rose is at the piano. He's been here twenty-five years and can play anything, can intuit the mood of the audience. Still, this is Great American Songbook territory, and he does a lot of George Gershwin and Cole Porter and Harold Arlen.

We are both born New Yorkers, and during a break, Rose and I fall into nostalgic conversation about Christmas in the city and the Lionel trains in the Toy Center near Madison Square Park.

When he returns to the piano, Rose glances at me and swings into Rodgers and Hart's 1925 standard "Manhattan"; a moment later, a few of us are humming along: "The great big city's a wondrous toy just made for a girl and boy. We'll turn Manhattan into an isle of joy!"

JUST NEXT DOOR

CAFÉ CARLYLE

As a kid, I loved ice-skating, especially at Wollman Rink, where, as you spun on the ice, you could see the city skyline. No more perfect expression of this exists than the lilting Modern Jazz Quartet tune "Skating in Central Park."

I actually saw the MJQ—John Lewis, Milt Jackson, Connie Kay, and Percy Heath—play it at Café Carlyle, the perfect venue for the most elegant of musicians.

The café evokes another city, that mythical one we all mourn, where everyone dances like Fred and Ginger. From 1968 to 2004, it was home to Bobby Short, who seemed to me the absolute reincarnation of Cole Porter. Witty and cool, Short made the café the quintessential New York supper club. I saw him only once.

On Monday nights at the café, another hard-core New Yorker, Woody Allen, plays the clarinet with his band. At the start of Allen's *Manhattan*, his character, trying to write about the city, says: "He adored New York City. He idolized it all out of proportion. . . . To him, no matter what the season was, this was still a town that existed in black and white and pulsated to the great tunes of George Gershwin. New York was his town, and it always would be."

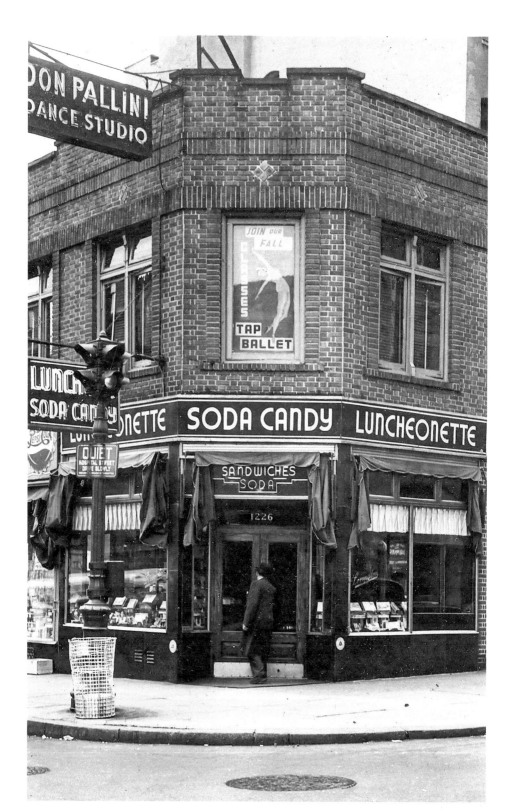

LEXINGTON CANDY SHOP

WHEN I WAS a kid, after a trip to the pediatrician, my mother took me for a grilled cheese. Or sometimes for a black-and-white ice cream soda. This was, as far as I can remember, a reward for not screaming too much when the doctor stuck a needle in me. I think my mother would have preferred a Scotch.

In any case, the Luncheonette on 83rd and Lexington was the place where a lot of New York children were taken. It is at the very heart of the world of doctors and dentists—hospitals, too. Even now, I sometimes meet somebody at the counter who goes to the same physician as I do. It gives the place a kind of village feel, even if you don't live on the Upper East Side. (Comparing docs is a sisterly sort of thing.) Nothing much has changed since I was little.

Owner John Philis (left) and his business partner, Bob Karcher, at the luncheonette.

Tami Naskos behind the counter at the Lexington Candy Shop. He and Soterios Philis founded the business in 1925.

Many of the servers have been here for decades. John Philis, who owns the shop, says, "We are surrounded by doctors and dentists here, and generation after generation come in with their families." He adds, "I love the sense of community that's invested in the business."

New Yorkers adore this kind of old-fashioned place with its malts and egg salad, though the way we rush to embrace new foods, you'd never know it; this is what produces the exquisite tension of the culinary life here in Manhattan, which can result in odd combinations—say, kale and cookies ice cream from By Chloe. Here on 83rd Street, I want only a root beer float. Luncheonette's customers hate new things.

When Philis replaced the wallpaper, for example, he undertook it with the care of a Renaissance restoration expert at the Met a few blocks away. But when he tried to change the phone number, there was trouble. The number had always been listed with its classic New York exchange of BUtterfield 8, which John O'Hara took as the title for his 1935 novel. (The movie version won Elizabeth Taylor an Oscar.) People were outraged; Philis went back to the original number.

The only change that Philis made was dropping both bologna and liverwurst sandwiches from the menu, along with the jelly omelets.

Otherwise, both in style and comestibles, this is the kind of luncheon-ette that was once ubiquitous in New York. You could call it the Last Luncheonette.

The shop is formally known as the Lexington Candy Shop—in its earliest incarnation, it was a chocolatier that sold other kinds of candy as well—but on the sign, it says Luncheonette. One of the front windows is jammed with old Coke bottles, the thick green glass covered with com-memorative logos from all over the world.

In the front are the cash register and a shelf with candy and gum for sale. The lunch counter runs the length of the narrow room. A row of stools provide ample opportunity for small children to spin, opposite a few booths for adults—art dealers, doctors, and, on weekends, divorced fathers and their kids. Behind the counter, archaeological objects on dis-play include a green 1942 Hamilton Beach malted machine with a malt dispenser next to it.

Order orange juice, and it's prepared on the spot using an old-fashioned juicer and served immediately. (Otherwise, according to Philis, it's never really fresh.) The best fresh lemonade in Manhattan is made here; there is a good lime rickey; and, nectar for the gods, coffee egg creams.

Vanilla and chocolate egg creams are still available in the city, but coffee egg creams are a rarity. This makes the Luncheonette, as the Michelin guide would say, worth the voyage. In fact, a couple of cus-tomers come from the West Side regularly for a coffee egg cream, one of them twice a day.

I sit down with John Philis for coffee in one of the green Naugahyde booths. A man with an open face and easy manner that keep customers coming back, he tells me that his grandfather Soterios Philis opened the luncheonette in 1925, just after arriving from Greece; it's remained at the same location ever since.

Although Philis got his master's degree in public administration at NYU, he eventually found that he missed the luncheonette where he had helped out since childhood. "When I was twelve, my father let me stand on a milk crate at the register," he says.

A couple of ladies are seated opposite us; after perusing the menu for twenty minutes, they decide to share a BLT. My mother and her best friend, in later life, always shared a sandwich between them.

Fried egg sandwiches, blueberry pancakes (and pecan pancakes and chocolate chip pancakes), and cinnamon raisin French toast, Philis sells them all. Egg salad, tuna melts, burgers and cheeseburgers, grilled cheese, and peanut butter and jelly, all the dishes and sandwiches that long, long before fancy food—before wraps and panini—everyone ate for lunch in New York City.

At another table is Philis's son Peter, who has also worked at the shop and is planning to open his own restaurant just up the block. This is a family affair, and that accounts for its charm.

Hanging on the walls, against the striped wallpaper, are photographs of regulars—locals who got engaged here, kids at birthday parties, the actor Tony Roberts. Woody Allen comes in. John Turturro shot a scene in *Fading Gigolo* (which starred Allen) at the Luncheonette. "I was in the last scene myself," Philis says. He looks the part of a jolly owner, the master of his domain, a character in a matinee. But then, in the Luncheonette, he has a venue that feels like the perfect set for a movie of another time on New York's Upper East Side.

ARTBAG

Up on Madison Avenue at Artbag, they'll clean, repair, or remake your favorite handbag (or purse, in American parlance): Hermès, Prada, Chanel, Gucci, or any bag you adore and can't part with. Artbag was founded in 1932 by Hillel Tenenbaum, a professor at the Fashion Institute of Technology. In 1993, it was purchased by his protégé, Donald Moore. Moore, having started at the shop as a young man, handed it over to his son, Chris Moore, establishing the great handbag dynasty of Madison Avenue.

THE JEWISH MUSEUM

New Yorkers possess their city in intricate and complicated ways that could well confound the most astute of anthropologists. In the Gilded Age, most of the museums on Fifth Avenue were still private mansions, palaces for the very rich. Among them is the Felix M. Warburg House, the building that now houses the Jewish Museum—one of my favorites. I like museums you can get your arms around: the Hispanic Society Museum & Library up on Audubon Terrace, the Cooper Hewitt, the Frick, the Morgan Library.

Originally the city's grandees lived downtown, near Washington Square Park. Nobody captures their move north, in the 1870s, better than Edith Wharton in *The Age of Innocence*. (Nobody captures anything about period New York better.) She wrote that one of the city's great matriarchs, Mrs. Manson Mingott, who was unconventional and very fat, "[p]ut the crowning touch to her audacities by building a large house of pale cream-colored stone . . . in an inaccessible wilderness near the Central Park. . . . The cream-colored house (supposed to be modeled on the private hotels of the Parisian aristocracy) was there as a visible proof of her moral courage; and she throned in it . . . as if there were nothing peculiar in living above 34th Street."

Mrs. Mingott would have approved of the Warburg House, if not of the inhabitants. (The society Wharton wrote about was bluntly anti-Semitic.) It was built in 1908 for Felix and Frieda Schiff Warburg. Mrs. Warburg (whose father worried that it was too fancy, that its display of wealth might provoke anti-Semitism) donated the house to the Jewish Theological Seminary of America as a home for its collection. It became the Jewish Museum in 1947. The museum has very good exhibitions and a fabulous shop, and it has Russ & Daughters— tying together the world of poor immigrant Jews from the Russian shtetls (like my father's family) who settled on the Lower East Side and that of the staggeringly wealthy and cultivated German Jews on the Upper East.

SCHALLER & WEBER

AS SOON AS I walk into Schaller & Weber, the little German grocery shop on Second Avenue and East 86th Street, I sense that something has changed. This is one of the very few remaining outposts of the old German neighborhood in what's still sometimes known as Yorkville. For years I regularly visited a friend nearby, and I'd always stop at Schaller for the Black Forest ham, the cucumber salad, maybe some of the dark breads—the pumpernickel and rye—and, of course, the sausages. In recent years, the shop, which opened more than ninety years ago, had started feeling a little bit dowdy, with a coating of dusty nostalgia; customers were perhaps seeking the Christmas stollen, marzipan figurines, and lingonberry jam of their youth.

Tony Weber (far right), one of the founders, with workers in the shop.

Weber (left) and cofounder Ferdinand Schaller with their first delivery truck, 1937.

But there's a buzz now, the shop seeming revitalized, peppy as a polka but contemporary as a Berlin rock club. Inside the small store, a steady stream of customers investigate a large selection of Austrian wines and German beers. Some Japanese tourists examine the gorgeous pink hams, salamis, cold cuts, the shelves full of house-made Düsseldorf-style mustard with horseradish; bemused, they examine a bottle of Berlin currywurst ketchup. A small lady in a large black fur hat who might have been shopping here almost since the place opened nods with reverence at the display case full of sausages—cheddar brats, knackwurst, blutwurst, Gelbwurst, even Irish bangers and Louisiana brand hot uncured sausages. It's all here.

My friend from Berlin, Alfred Heilhecker, concurs: "Every year, I come to the city for a visit, and when I discovered Schaller & Weber, I was so glad that I no longer had to smuggle in Nürnberger bratwurst and Weisswurst for my friends in New York," he says. "Their product is so authentic and of such quality that I can't get better in Berlin. If you like cured and smoked meat (and sauerkraut), it's the only address in the city. They are very friendly and explain to customers who don't know how to cook their stuff how to do it."

Two of Schaller & Weber's experienced countermen: Jacek Danielak (right) and Brendan Cunningham—manager Chris Cunningham's son.

In the shop, there is the brisk sound of hungry shoppers. The butcher counter is stocked with gorgeous steaks and pork chops; there are fresh baguettes and veggies. Schaller also sells a marvelous fried chicken. "The secret," Jeremy Schaller says, "is that we put it in the fryers where the pork was cooked."

In his early forties, blue-eyed, and very charming, Jeremy is the third generation of his family to own the shop, and he has turned it into a complete gourmet grocery while keeping the original sausages and ambiance that have always existed. His grandfather Ferdinand, who had been a butcher in Germany, opened the shop in 1937, and it was later run by Jeremy's father, Frank, and Frank's brother, Ralph. But instead of going into the business, Jeremy went to college and into the fashion industry. Eventually, though, he realized how much he missed the shop where he had played as a kid and later worked as a teenager. "Come back," said his uncle. And he did.

As with so many of the best food shops in New York—Di Palo's in Little Italy, Russ & Daughters on the Lower East Side—at Schaller

The interior of Schaller & Weber, packed with sausages, hams, cheeses, jams, cookies, marzipan, and beer. In its new iteration, the shop is so popular that it needs a ticket system to keep the lines in check.

& Weber, the generational continuity has provided an enormous transfusion of ambition, interest, passion; it has meant better and more varied products without a loss of essence, that Germanness shared by everyone who speaks the mother tongue and loves a great sausage.

By the end of the nineteenth century, New York City had the third largest German-speaking population outside of Vienna and Berlin, mostly in Little Germany (what is now the East Village). By the start of the twentieth century, most of the Germans had moved uptown to Yorkville. The area from East 79th Street to East 96th Street, Third Avenue to the East River, was known as Germantown, and 86th Street was often referred to as Sauerkraut Boulevard. There were Hungarians, Austrians, Czechs, and Poles, and this part of New York City was a world of schnitzel, strudel, and coffee mit Schlag; of the Café Geiger; of German movie theaters and beer halls and dance halls. By 1938, the *New Yorker Staats-Zeitung* newspaper sold eighty thousand or more copies a day. There were also Nazis.

Jeremy Schaller, the third generation of Schallers to own the shop.

During the 1930s, Yorkville was the New York base of the German-American Bund. These were American Nazis who marched on 86th Street and rallied in Madison Square Garden. After the war started, the reaction was so ferocious that innocent Germans living in the States, including Ferdinand Schaller, were sent to internment camps, sometimes for years. When the war ended, Schaller returned to New York and his shop, and his sons subsequently took over. Some decades later, it was Jeremy's turn.

"Jeremy gets tradition," says Chris Cunningham, who has worked for Schaller for twenty-five years. "When he painted one of the walls black, I thought he was out of his mind. But when he brought the company into the twenty-first century, he got it right."

Jeremy added a Stube next door to the shop, a sort of brat bar where you can grab a grilled bratwurst on a pretzel bun (there's another Stube in the Essex Market downtown). This was once the main entrance, and you can still see the huge black wheel and enormous gears used to slide sides of meat from trucks at curbside into the back, where butchers turned them into sausage. These days, everything—the sausage, the charcuterie—is made at the Schaller plant in Pennsylvania.

Down a flight of stairs is a small private room where Jeremy and I share some cold cuts from the shop—salamis, hams, liverwurst, bologna, and cheese—along with heavy dark bread (I like the really dense bread that's the shape and weight of a little nuclear weapon), all laid out on a low table. I've always loved liverwurst; when I was young, we ate liverwurst sandwiches on rye from Ruben's deli on 10th Street. There's also Landjäger, a kind of German jerky, in case you need something to help you survive your next hike in the Alps (put the dried meat in the pocket of your lederhosen), and delicious cold pilsner that's always on tap at the Schaller Stube.

Frank Schaller, who lives in California now, says, "I think Schaller & Weber has been at this location since 1937 because we believe in the importance of our heritage, the vitality of New York City, and the quality of our products." There's really no greater testament to a good sausage than praise from a German native; says Alfred, "When I'm in New York, I always head for Schaller & Weber first thing, to prevent an inevitable bout of Heimweh (a kind of melancholy homesickness)."

PHILIP ROTH AND THE CHOPPED HERRING SANDWICH

———

BARNEY GREENGRASS

AFRIEND ONCE TOLD me that she had stalked Philip Roth at Barney Greengrass. She knew it was where he sometimes ate lox and eggs. Obsessed with the writer (his books, his looks), all she got for her trouble was breakfast. I feel sad that she never got to meet—or do anything else—with him. Philip Roth is gone now. Still, in his honor, I made the trek to the Upper West Side and the famous appetizing store and restaurant where the smoked sturgeon is reputedly the best in town.

New York is the most intensely tribal city I know. A lifelong downtown denizen, I made my first visit to Barney Greengrass only in 2019. As I walked uptown from the subway, past the brownstones sleeping in the sun on 87th Street, I was in a different New York: more residential, more

filled with gorgeous buildings mostly built in the early twentieth century. The legendary—and that's no hyperbole—shop and restaurant has been on Amsterdam Avenue at 87th Street for more than ninety years. Before that, it was in Harlem, when Harlem had a large Jewish population, for over twenty years.

BARNEY GREENGRASS, declares the huge red sign out front. Inside, the store has the original Art Deco-ish baked-enamel-and-white-porcelain counter, the mirrors, the detailing, the little ledge maybe a foot or two wide where customers can enjoy a quick meal. All of it has been left virtually unchanged since 1929.

The display cases are crammed with smoked fish, herring, gefilte fish, potato salad, blintzes, and latkes; the marble counters are piled high with bagels and bialys, babka, rugelach, black-and-white cookies—all the things beloved of New York Jews. Of course you can get this all downtown, too, but Philip Roth was an Upper West Side guy.

Operation Shylock is one of Roth's wildest and funniest novels. In it, his narrator (who might or might not be the real Roth, as well) notes that on occasion, he would come down to Manhattan from Connecticut to satisfy his "inextinguishable appetite for the chopped-herring salad as it was unceremoniously served up (that was the ceremony)."

I love Roth's books for the brilliant writing, the language, the characters, all of it, but also because even in the darkest novels, the characters, the narrator, the writer, seem so alive, so vivid and funny, and so hungry! (Who can forget the fresh fruit in a dedicated fridge at his rich, suburban girlfriend's house in *Goodbye, Columbus*, or the jar of wildly expensive Tiptree Little Scarlet strawberry preserve that Mickey Sabbath swipes from his rich Upper West Side friends in *Sabbath's Theater*? Not to mention that family dinner of liver in *Portnoy's Complaint*!)

The shop's owner, Gary Greengrass, grandson of the founder, says of Roth, "When he came in, we used to kibitz, and he signed a book for me."

Behind the shop is the restaurant that serves breakfast and lunch to its obsessively devoted clientele that has included, in addition to Roth, Nora Ephron, Jerry Seinfeld, and Anthony Bourdain. (To mark Bourdain's passing, an empty table was set with his favorite Nova Scramble—lox and eggs—and a toasted bialy, as if waiting for the prophet to return.)

More from *Operation Shylock*, where Philip Roth writes of a somewhat mysterious character: "Smilesburger had chosen as the site for our editorial meeting a Jewish food store on Amsterdam Avenue, specializing in smoked fish, that served breakfast and lunch on a dozen Formica-topped tables in a room adjacent to the bagel and bialy counter and that looked as though, years back, when someone got the bright idea to 'modernize,' the attempt at redecoration had been sensibly curtailed halfway through."

The value of vintage is not lost on Gary Greengrass, who tells me he has gone to a lot of trouble to preserve the shop's original decor, even hiring an artist to touch up the drab brown and beige wallpaper with its pictures of old New Orleans.

This is a store that has real cultural chops. The Upper West Side has been heavily Jewish from the time German Jews arrived at the turn of the last century; more European Jews came in the 1930s, fleeing Hitler. Barney Greengrass has always been a gathering place, a place to eat and gossip and maybe make a deal.

Now the neighborhood is full of comfortable writers and editors, not to mention lawyers and TV executives who can't live without the Greengrass sturgeon and nova. In *Operation Shylock*, Roth pondered this changing world: "Now, of course, what was once the ordinary fare of the Jewish masses had become an exotic stimulant for Upper West Siders two and three generations removed from the great immigration and just getting by as professionals in Manhattan on annual salaries that, a century earlier, would have provided daily banquets all year long for every last Jew in Galicia."

Once, smoked sturgeon was the food of czars more than of the shtetl Jews from whom so many of us are descended, including the Greengrass family. Barney Greengrass was one of the earliest shopkeepers to spread the word and the sturgeon. WE SHIP OUR PRODUCTS ANYWHERE IN THE US OVERNIGHT DELIVERY, says the sign on the shop window. "My grandfather would ship his smoked fish by US mail Parcel Post," says Gary Greengrass. "There was a label that said, 'If not delivered in three days, forget it.'"

LEFT TO RIGHT: Actor Eli Wallach, Moe Greengrass (son of founder Barney), and actor Zero Mostel during filming of *The Angel Levine*, 1969.

Great smoked kippers, in addition to the smoked sturgeon and fixings, are on offer at Barney Greengrass.

In 1938, Barney sent ten pounds of sturgeon to FDR in the White House for Thanksgiving dinner. James J. Frawley, an early-twentieth-century New York judge, gave Barney Greengrass his name "the Sturgeon King." Barney Greengrass has the raffish air of a place in which deals have been done and politics played. The most discreet of power breakfasts are held here in relative obscurity, as if it were an Italian social club with lox. Says Gary, "I introduced the late New Jersey senator Frank Lautenberg to Philip Roth one day, two guys from Newark."

In one episode of *Billions*—a show that now has its own New York restaurant blog—Paul Giamatti, as the endlessly hustling corrupt New York attorney general, when seeking a favor, finds the police commissioner eating breakfast at Barney Greengrass. The very tense conversation is held over bagels.

On the afternoon when I settle in at a table, a woman wearing a tie-dyed tunic goes past. Opposite me are a mother and son and a couple of women with grandkids. "I love this place because it binds the

BARNEY GREENGR[ASS]
The STURGEON KING

TOP QUALITY DAIRY PRODUCTS
SOLD HERE EXCLUSIVELY AT ...

HITS
SPOT

OUR FAMOUS HOME MADE
PICKLED HERRING

generations," says Joey, a waiter who has been here since 1997. Gary Greengrass agrees, which is why he joined the family business in the first place.

The store in the 1940s.

Gary went to NYU for broadcast journalism, but he realized he was destined instead to be prince to the Sturgeon King—until he ascended the throne himself. The perfect front man, Gary has never met a joke he didn't like telling, but he also knows his fish. For years he worked with his father, Moe (son of Barney); some mornings, at three, they would visit the smokers who turned fresh fish into exquisite smoked sturgeon. It was then that he learned his sturgeon.

Lake sturgeon were pretty much gone thirty-five years ago; most of the fish is now farmed, Gary says, noting, "The flavor is actually better. The variations in the fish—each one has an individual quality—are what give it its texture and flavor.'"

I turn to my copy of *Operation Shylock*. In it, Roth (or his stand-in) asks for "the chopped-herring salad on a lightly toasted onion bagel.

Owner Gary Greengrass behind
a pile of hamantaschen.

Tomato on the side," adding, "And bring me a glass of orange juice."
I skip the juice and order the bagel, and with it a side of the exquisite
smoked sturgeon. I eat and go on reading.

In the novel, Roth recalls the aromas of the Newark shop where, in
the 1940s, his family shopped for Sunday breakfast: "the bitter fragrance
of vinegar, of onions, of whitefish and red herring, of everything pickled, peppered, salted, smoked, soaked, stewed, marinated, and dried,
smells with a lineage that, like these stores themselves, more than likely
led straight back through the shtetl to the medieval ghetto and the
nutrients of those who lived frugally and could not afford to dine à la
mode, the diet of sailors and common folk, for whom the flavor of the
ancient preservatives was life."

THE HUNGARIAN PASTRY SHOP

I**T'S HARD TO** think of a better example than the Hungarian Pastry Shop of what makes one love a city, a neighborhood, a place," says the distinguished poet and writer Rachel Hadas. "That 'what' is hard to define but easy to recognize and to remember. It's a combination: the location and the people, the coffee and the weather, the croissants and the conversations."

This is a coffee shop beloved for decades by writers and Columbia and Barnard students and professors, who have eaten delicious flaky croissants, drunk the "Hungarian coffee" (drip coffee with almond flavoring and a mountain of whipped cream), and scrawled their politics on the bathroom walls.

At this small café with rickety chairs opposite St. John the Divine, New York's grandest cathedral, the bathroom graffiti got so bad at one

point that owner Philip Binioris repainted the whole room. He said, "The discourse had become aggressive and ugly, and the outpouring of venom included swastikas. People are capable of more enlightened debate."
I love the idea of a café where enlightened debate is the driving force.

The exterior of the shop in the late 1970s (above) and today (opposite).

There's no Wi-Fi, and the lighting is not great, but the coffee refills are free, and the pastries are large and sweet. The Hungarian Pastry Shop is about the atmosphere; it's about the kind of vibes people once found in the cafés of Paris or Heidelberg or, indeed, Budapest. You hang out here, you attain a kind of intellectual street cred. Ask any Columbia alum about it, and you unleash a torrent of postgrad nostalgia.

It is also a neighborhood place where local families and kids hang out and eat up the apricot linzer tarts and pains au chocolat. It hasn't really changed much since 1976, when Philip's parents, Panagiotis and Wendy Binioris, bought the shop from a Hungarian couple who had opened it around 1960. "My father started working as a busboy at Symposium, another restaurant, in the early 1970s, after emigrating from Greece," Philip says. Gradually Panagiotis worked his way up to waiter and eventually, with his wife and a couple of Greek pals, bought the café.

Rachel Hadas recalls asking Wendy and Panagiotis Binioris how they managed with four children under the age of six, including Philip. Says

Hadas, "Wendy replied, 'I have no idea. I can't remember.'" But manage she did. The family seemed harmonious, and for countless denizens of Morningside Heights, the pastry shop was always a friendly and familiar place of refuge and peace.

The Hungarian Pastry Shop has long been a family affair, for both the owners and the customers. Philip worked in the café after school from the time he was thirteen, and in 2012, when his father retired, he took it over. As he chats, he stops to wave at a friend, then hurries to make a cappuccino. "It's our daily customers who make us what we are," he says. "They really love the place, and they really keep us honest. It is a regular occurrence for us to have someone walk up to the counter and tell us, 'It's exactly the same as it was ten-twenty-thirty years ago.' That's a big deal in a city that changes so quickly."

"It's the way the place changed constantly but also remained reliably and reassuringly the same, so that the very changes were part of what one expected," Hadas adds. "Philip, whom I remember as a small boy, is now a tall, bespectacled father. Waitresses come and go. Children grow up; Cathedral and Columbia and Barnard students graduate. In the winter, opening the door of the pastry shop would let in a blast of cold air, but it was warm and cozy inside. In the spring and summer and fall, one hoped for a seat outside, but even inside, the long narrow room was a good place to be." Hadas pauses. "Mornings, when the low light streams in from the east across the cathedral close, were and still are my favorite times there, before the place gets too crowded—though it's sometimes hard to find a table by 8:30," she says.

Andrew Delbanco, author of the extraordinary book *The War Before the War*, recalls the café as a cozy shelter on winter mornings where he and his wife, Dawn, would stop after they dropped their daughter, Yvonne, off at school. "Back in the '80s and early '90s, the Hungarian became a sort of writing studio for me—a place where one could somehow be sociable and focused on work at the same time," Andrew explains. "I wasn't the only writer who developed a language of nods and waves that signaled to friends whether one was there to work or to schmooze. In my case, I became completely dependent on the almond horn pastry—the crunchier the better—which got my working day off to a great start!"

This is a community in an intensely tribal New York way where everyone is interconnected. People who have spent not years but decades at the Hungarian Pastry Shop are as protective of it as they are of their own children. In good weather, they sit outside and watch tourists taking pictures of the cathedral across the street.

Woody Allen set a scene in *Husbands and Wives* in the Hungarian Pastry Shop, with him as a needy writing teacher and Juliette Lewis as the student who tells him he's not as good as he thinks. The café seemed perfectly placed for the episode. Hadas says, "I had memorable coffee hours with the poets Jane Cooper and, later, Rachel Wetzsteon, both of whom lived around the corner on 110th Street, both now deceased."

I'm sitting at a table in the café eating pastry with Yvonne and Dawn Delbanco (who helped me judge the dim sum at Jing Fong—see page 29). Yvonne went to school with Philip Binioris's sister, Sofia. "Their father would allow us to 'help' make cookies—I think it was the raspberry and apricot linzer tarts," Yvonne says. "We were actually allowed to sell some of the better-looking creations."

Rachel Hadas says, "It has been a regular meeting place for morning coffee and endless refreshing conversation about children, parents, husbands, school, literature, art, life, and death." Hadas is Dawn Delbanco's best friend. "In the spring of 2019, my husband and I made the acquaintance of Simone, the infant daughter of Yvonne Delbanco and her wife, Emilia Hermann. Where else would we meet but at the pastry shop?"

Philip stops by to chat for a moment and then shows me the wall across from the pastry counter, featuring books by authors who have written them in the café. "What I love most about the book wall is the variety," says Philip. "Just like the city we live in, there is a little bit of everything on that wall, from self-help to academic works, fiction, non-fiction and philosophy, and children's books—award winners and not, they all belong, and they are all part of our community."

ACROSS THE STREET

THE CATHEDRAL OF ST. JOHN THE DIVINE

I once met a stonemason at St. John the Divine. He was in the process of making repairs to the great Gothic Revival cathedral. He told me that working at St. John felt like being employed at an ancient cathedral, that there was no other place like it in New York City for his trade.

St. John the Divine, the seat of the Episcopal archdiocese of New York, has a poet's corner and a deanery; it always puts me in mind of one of the grand English cathedrals, the kind of enclosed world in its own right described by

Anthony Trollope in *The Chronicles of Barsetshire*.

But this is New York, and locals love the place not just for its astonishing stained glass and its imposing scale but also for its concerts, political events, and magnificent funerals. How I long to have been at Duke Ellington's, where Ella Fitzgerald sang "In My Solitude." Most of all, everybody cherishes St. John the Divine for the annual Blessing of the Animals. This has included dogs and cats, of course, but also horses, a cow, a pair of doves, and a pig.

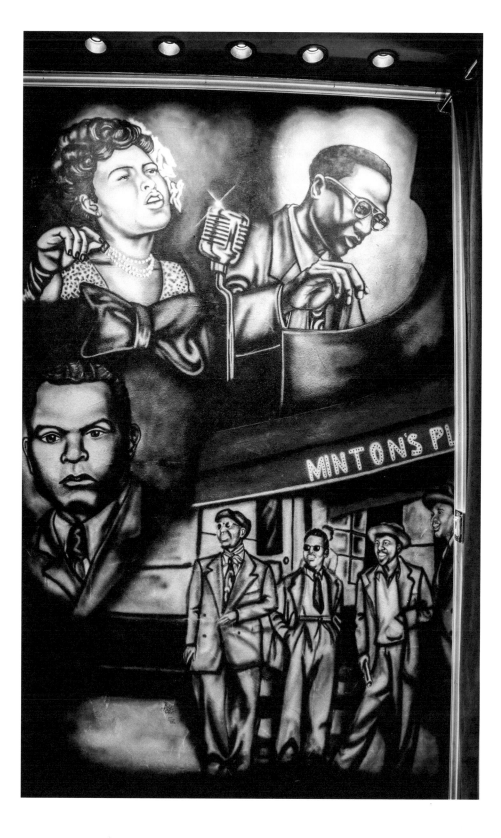

MINTON'S PLAYHOUSE

IN THE EARLY 1940s, Ella Fitzgerald, who was already a superstar in the world of swing music, suddenly and brilliantly changed course. The girl who had made her name with "A-Tisket, A-Tasket" became a jazz musician who could bop with the boys. And she could sometimes be found at Minton's Playhouse in Harlem. Says Tony Bennett, "She knew how to improvise better than anybody I ever listened to. Just like an instrumentalist would take a jazz solo, she would do that vocally, and it would be perfection." No one—with the possible exception of Louis Armstrong, who was, in a way, one of her musical mentors—could ever scat like Ella.

Minton's Playhouse is the last of the great Harlem jazz clubs. Taking our orders at Minton's early one Sunday evening, the French waiter,

LEFT TO RIGHT: Thelonious Monk, Howard McGhee, Roy Eldridge, and Teddy Hill, outside Minton's Playhouse, 1947.

improbably named Karl Smith, tells me that when he got to New York, he was determined "to do something very American." For a Frenchman, nothing could be more American than jazz and Harlem. Karl smiles as he looks over at the bandstand, where the musicians are tuning up and the grand piano shines, and then he darts away to get our drinks.

Minton's! With an almost impossibly legendary name, this little club on West 118th Street opened by sax player Henry Minton in 1938 is where bebop was born and the musical world swung off its axis. There, a few young guys—Thelonious Monk, Dizzy Gillespie, Charlie Parker—invented a music that was dissonant, complex, strange, hard, seductive, and gorgeous in a cerebral way.

World War II was on. The big bands and Harlem ballrooms where people went to dance were on their way out; the new modern jazz was made for small clubs where customers listened with the kind of attention they might give to Bach. But even with his most demanding music, the joyous Dizzy could seduce any audience, calling out "Salt peanuts, salt peanuts" when he played his legendary piece called . . . "Salt Peanuts." The music defined cool.

Arriving with a friend on the quiet Harlem street earlier that day, the pink neon sign alight outside the club, I feel I might actually see Monk, who was also Minton's house pianist, as he is pictured in a famous photograph: outside the club with some other musicians, smiling, wearing a too-big pin-striped suit and that jaunty beret, a smoke in one hand.

Alas, Monk is long gone. We head inside the narrow room, painted burnt orange, the bar up front, the rows of banquettes in back a plush yellowish orange; the tables are draped with white linen, and the subtle lighting gilds the whole place.

Behind the bar, a suave bartender is shaking cocktails for a few early patrons. Back at our table, our waiter delivers drinks, an "Ella" for me, a "Satchmo" for my friend. I'm wondering if I want a "Kind of Blue" appetizer, though I'm not sure I see Miles Davis—who played at Minton's when he was very young—as a mussels in white wine kind of guy; he was always more Beluga caviar and Dom Pérignon.

On the walls behind the banquettes are William Gottlieb's photos—Monk at the piano, Charlie Parker, Dizzy Gillespie, Charlie Christian with his guitar. Billie Holiday is there, too, her signature gardenia behind one ear. All the rich black-and-white images feel both elusive and eternal, glamorous, melancholy, and in the moment. It makes me think of writer Whitney Balliett's great line about jazz, that it's "the sound of surprise."

At the far end of the lovely room is the bandstand. Tonight is a regular Sunday set known as Singer Meets Saxophonist, and sax player Christopher McBride is chatting with his band. A black grand piano shines in a spotlight.

"Everyone I love in jazz is dead," says my companion, cranky, bearing down on a fat and juicy burger and ordering more wine. And then McBride rips into a Sonny Rollins original, spilling choruses from his alto sax. My friend looks up, diverted from his burger. "My God," he says, "this guy is a master; he's the real thing."

McBride roars on, radiating joy, as vivid as his Hawaiian shirt; his pianist, the stunningly good Jonathan Edward Thomas, and the drummer, Curtis Nowosad from Winnipeg (Winnipeg? My mother was from Winnipeg, but jazz this good?), swap complex patterns; the vocalist Cedric Easton coaxes rhythm from a wood box and an abacus.

Drawing on older traditions—call-and-response, gospel, Chicago, New Orleans—McBride makes me think of Cannonball Adderley. I love

Photographs of the original
bebop musicians, including
Charlie Christian and Billie
Holiday, hang above the booths.

Cannonball, and I love McBride, this young guy who, in his mid-thirties, is part of a network of fabulous young jazz musicians in New York, many of whom often play at Minton's. He is doing for the audience what great music should do: turning them on.

Over the bandstand is the famous Minton's mural, painted in 1948; four musicians, suspended in time, sit in a Harlem hotel room. In the picture, there's a bottle of port on the dresser, a girl asleep on the bed, facedown.

By the second set, there's a crowd—couples, families, good-looking mostly, a mix of white and Black, locals and tourists. McBride tells the audience, "This is Harlem. If you like what we do, just holler 'All Day Long.'"

So we call it out. We're all tourists now. In a 1959 *Esquire* piece, Ralph Ellison describes how in that same decade, young Europeans came to

Saxophonist Christopher McBride and his group performing at Minton's.

Minton's as to a shrine in the way young Americans in Paris went to Café de Flore or Les Deux Magots.

Over the years, Minton's closed down, collected dust, then was reopened but failed. In 2013, Richard Parsons, ex-CEO of Time Warner and CBS, took it over. Parsons told me that as a teenager in Brooklyn, taking a date to a Manhattan jazz club made him feel grown up, and he thought, *One day, I'll own a great supper club.* He has always loved the music and is now responsible, at least in part, for the flourishing jazz scene in Harlem. I mentioned to Parsons that I was probably hanging around the Village Vanguard about the same time he was.

The music, the clubs, the idea of it all, is, for me, wrapped in a web of nostalgia for both my youth and a disappearing New York; melancholy, too, because so much of the music, even the sharpest, most angular bebop always seems tinged with the blues.

Minton's

MINTON'S PLAYHOUSE

Minton's was the place where Bebop was born, the place, really, where the foundations of modern jazz were established. Founded in 1938 by the saxophonist Henry Minton (from whom the establishment took its name) Minton's Playhouse, became over the next decade, the setting for a revolution in jazz.

Duke Ellington, Louis Armstrong, Ella Fitzgerald, Billie Holiday, Benny Goodman, Coleman Hawkins, Lester Young, Johnny Hodges, Ben Webster, Sarah Vaughan, Carmen McRea, Billy Eckstine, Erroll Garner, Gene Krupa, Miles Davis, Art Tatum, Bill Evans and Art Blakey, all played at Minton's.

While Minton's is most famous for the seminal role it played in the Bebop revolution of the 1940s, the club had a vital existence through the early 1960s as a magnet for musicians who wanted to jam and continued to operate until 1974, when a fire led to the abandonment of the Cecil Hotel where Minton's was housed.

Now the Jews, in recognition of its significance in American history and culture, Minton's Playhouse has been listed on both the National and the New York State Register of Historic Places.

WEST END

ELLINGTON

Teddy Powell

MINTON'S

JAZZ JAM

Christopher McBride and his guys are still playing, and now they're at the finale, a pair of Beatles songs: "Blackbird" and "Come Together" are refashioned as soaring, stamping celebrations of the power of music to thrill and unite. The crowd is on its feet, arms waving, as McBride and his band dance through the audience to lead a joyous celebration that recalls a New Orleans Mardi Gras procession, an invitation to join in and come together to defy the divisions of a fractured America.

All day long!

AFTER THE SHOW

SYLVIA'S

After a night at the Harlem clubs, musicians often go to Sylvia's for chicken and waffles. It makes for a hearty breakfast after a gig—accompanied by plenty of drinks—that lasted until dawn.

All that smothered and fried chicken, fried fish, cornbread with butter, those grits and mashed potatoes, the red velvet cake and cobblers—the food at Sylvia's fills you up for days.

I love the place. People are always saying it's too touristy, that I should go to the new hip Harlem restaurants, of which there are many, some of them terrific, among them Maison Harlem, Corner Social, and Marcus Samuelsson's Red Rooster. Sylvia's, though, has history, and a friendly staff who really want you to enjoy—to overeat if you want, to delight in the food. If it draws in plenty of tourists, it is also the most local of all the restaurants.

At lunch one day with a couple of Harlem friends, I'm drinking iced tea and eating chicken and greens, and in walks Charles Rangel. The leonine head, the swept-back silver hair, the smile—this is a real Harlem celebrity, its congressman for decades, a New Yorker among New Yorkers. My friend Curtis introduces me. Mr. Rangel shakes my hand. I ask how he likes Sylvia's. "I made my reputation here; I was Sylvia's lawyer," he says. "He was also," Curtis says softly, "the lawyer for Malcolm X."

FLAMEKEEPERS HAT CLUB

INSIDE THE STYLISH shop on 121st Street and Frederick Douglass Boulevard, there are hats: Hats displayed individually, like precious art objects, in gorgeous greens and purples. Newsboy caps and cashmere baseball caps and flat caps in Donegal tweed (I love the one in black cherry), stacked in mouthwatering piles. I've always loved hats, especially men's hats, so for me FlameKeepers was a fabulous find. My own particular favorite is an elegant Panama.

There are porkpie hats, the kind Buster Keaton wore, and Gene Hackman, in *The French Connection*. But the king of the porkpie was the great tenor sax jazz musician Lester "Prez" Young, who always wore one. Charles Mingus wrote a tune about him called "Goodbye Pork Pie

Men in boater hats attending
Marcus Garvey's UNIA (Universal
Negro Improvement Association)
parade in Harlem, 1920.

FlameKeepers offers a vivid
and cutting-edge take on the
classic fedora.

Hat" in 1959. Dizzy Gillespie might have popped in to FlameKeepers
for one of the berets he sported—and maybe Duke Ellington for one of
owner Marc Williamson's magnificent top hats.

Straw boaters with red and blue ribbons look as if they might have
been worn by Edwardian dandies rowing on the lake in Central Park.
Fedoras come in every color—I like steel gray for Bogie and a rich
plummy black for Shaft. Williamson is especially keen on both styles.
"For many men, regardless of their age, fedoras represent a rite of pas-
sage from adolescence into manhood," he says, recalling that back in the
day, boys wore caps, but men wore hats. As for the boaters, Williamson
feels that anyone wearing a boater today *"absolutely* has some level of
confidence and dares to tread where many won't."

In old photographs of Harlem from the 1920s, all the men look
very sharp, and many of them are wearing boaters. Right through the
decades, Harlem has always seemed synonymous with hats and with a
certain masculine style. Hats took a bit of a downturn when JFK memorably did not wear one to his inauguration. But with the age of the
hipster, they made a comeback. Marc Williamson was ready.

Owner Marc Williamson surrounds his customers with warmth, energy, and color.

In fact, though, Williamson more or less fell into hats. He grew up with his mother and sister in Woodside, Queens, where he still lives with his two young daughters. "As a student, I was not particularly interested in fashion—I was doing music—but I was dating a woman who went to FIT, and I needed a job," he says. Perusing the FIT bulletin board, he noticed a job posting for a stock person at the JJ Hat Center. After three interviews, he got the position. It was 1996. JJ Hat Center, which has been around since 1911, was the go-to place for an enormous selection of classic headgear.

Eventually Williamson became the manager and was responsible for most of the buying. He learned to fit hats and also to design them. His ambition was to buy the store. "But that it did not happen was a blessing," Williamson says. Self-funded, he eventually opened his own shop on 121st Street on August 30, 2014—he remembers the date precisely. "The timing was lucky," he says. "Hats were suddenly on, and I gave my voice to what were the hat game wars." He smiles. "Hipsters, Brooklyn folk, Lower East Side people—everyone was wearing hats."

These days, FlameKeepers sells hats to business-men and entertainers. Women love the hats here, too. Williamson works with factories all over the world, often buying hat skeletons (the frame or "bones"

"When you visit FlameKeepers, our goal is to show you what Harlem feels like," says Marc Williamson.

of a hat) and finishing them himself. The shop also offers one-of-a-kind satchels, canvas and leather carryalls, silk pocket squares, a limited-edition flask, and hat jacks—wooden devices to keep your hat in shape.

A big part of FlameKeepers' appeal is Marc Williamson himself. Handsome and charming, he is also deeply welcoming. The shop acts as a kind of social gathering place for locals. "Marc is one of the kinder old souls I've met," says Benjamin McCauley, a biomedical researcher at Mount Sinai and a Harlem resident. Eighty percent of the time when McCauley goes to the shop—part of his weekend routine—it's to see friends. "No matter what's going on, there's no place that feels more welcoming than Marc's store," he says.

McCauley also loves the way the hats in Williamson's shop constantly evolve according to the season. "His custom pieces are truly artworks," he says. When he wanted a hat for his father, Williamson asked him what his dad was like. His answer: a bourbon distiller in Virginia who loves guns. Says McCauley, "Marc ended up purchasing a leather bandolier he'd found and a pocketknife that looked like a shotgun shell and sewed them onto the side of the hat. It was absolutely perfect, and my dad always wears it when he sees his friends."

To McCauley and many other locals and visitors, FlameKeepers is the real flavor of Harlem. And not just Harlem, but New York City. You feel that Marc Williamson, a born-and-bred New Yorker, could well be the first in a dynasty, that his hats will last, that in twenty or thirty years, people will still be coming by to see the great hat merchant of Harlem.

A MILE NORTH

ABYSSINIAN BAPTIST CHURCH

On a Sunday morning in Harlem, crowds are streaming toward West 138th Street and the Abyssinian Baptist Church.

This famous Christian house of worship has been tightly woven into the fabric of the city since as far back as 1808, when a group of Ethiopian merchants who refused to accept segregated seating at the First Baptist Church formed a new church nearby, in lower Manhattan.

The church eventually moved north, along with the city's Black population. Dedicated in 1923, the current building is a prepossessing Gothic and Tudor structure. It is one of the great powerhouse New York churches, the biggest Black church in the city, with a world-class choir, and a place where any candidate for mayor or even president has to pay a visit. This is the church where Adam Clayton Powell Sr. was the pastor; his son, Adam Clayton Powell Jr., was the first Black congressman from New York.

To watch New York at prayer is to see what is a quintessentially commerce-driven town in a different light. The Reverend Calvin O. Butts welcomes the congregants and calls out the names of visiting family and friends of friends. The crowd of nearly a thousand seems like a tight-knit community, especially on this morning when babies—all of them exquisitely dressed—are brought in for a blessing. That is followed by the choir and the whole congregation singing "This Little Light of Mine." And then everyone shakes hands, and my friends and I head to Ruby's Vintage, a block away, for brunch.

———

CHARLES' COUNTRY PAN FRIED CHICKEN

IT'S SEVEN O'CLOCK on a February evening in Harlem, and at Charles' Country Pan Fried Chicken, a faint aroma wafts out on the cold night air. At 132nd Street and Frederick Douglass Boulevard, Charles' is a storefront restaurant, nothing fancy; inside, there's a trio of long tables and the counter where you order. Charles Gabriel, chef and owner, is downstairs in the kitchen frying up the chicken.

It all feels like a throwback, a time before fast-food and chain restaurants—both low-end and high—shut down the ma-and-pa eateries and stole their livelihood. There are those of us, though, who willingly stand in line because the few remaining places like Charles' give New York a beating human heart and make it worth living in.

There are historians who claim that fried chicken originally came from Scotland. To most Harlemites—to most New Yorkers, in fact—it's a dish that in large part came to New York from the South during the Great Migration and became a staple; in Manhattan, some of the best of it has been cooked by Charles Gabriel for decades.

His is the platonic ideal of fried chicken, the essence of the bird: moist, tender meat, mouthwatering in its crispy delicately seasoned crust; every batch is seasoned three times, then constantly turned as it's gently panfried in soybean oil, which is low in saturated fat (in case you've been reading health columns that say fried chicken can kill you); anyhow, this is chicken I'd die for. Other fans include Whoopi Goldberg, Danny Glover, and Wesley Snipes, all of whom have regularly ordered chicken from Charles. Charles Gabriel has been written up by the *New York Times* and *The New Yorker*. On a recent Super Bowl Sunday, the restaurant sold two thousand pieces of fried chicken.

Coming up from the kitchen, Charles is holding a pan of freshly fried chicken. For regulars, he has a ready smile, and he greets an older woman by name, kisses a little girl in a pink winter jacket.

"Harlem has a lot of love for Charles," says Karen Murray, who, with her husband, Curtis Archer, has come to meet me for dinner. The little girl in pink announces that she loves the chicken.

"It's seasoned to perfection, a component often missing in fried chicken," says Karen, who admits that as one of the few Black people born in Vermont, she may not have as much fried chicken cred as some-one from the South or Harlem; still, she knows a delicious chicken breast when she tastes it.

To tell the truth, Karen and I have both been on no-carb diets since New Year's, but one bite of the chicken and we're both lost to it. You eat it with your hands. The skin, as it slides off, has a lovely crunch; the juicy flesh gives way in your mouth. People still waiting in line eye us enviously. You get a couple of sides with your chicken: mac and cheese, yams, okra, collard greens, black-eyed peas, white rice. Charles serves smothered pork chops, oxtail, and barbecue, too, but most people come here for the chicken.

Charles Gabriel serving
customers at his restaurant.

"Just a buttermilk-and-egg wash overnight," says Charles. "Dip it in flour, salt and pepper, then a few secret extras," he adds with a smile. "That's all," he says, as if anyone could do it. But no one else has invested a lifetime of history, passion, bad times and good in making it perfect. Nobody else has a collection of old cast-iron pans, seasoned over decades, to fry their chicken in.

Born in rural North Carolina, one of twenty-one kids, Charles learned to cook from his mother. His own two sons live in the South now, and both cook. I ask him if he might go back. "I have memories," he says plainly. "We lived on a plantation. My parents were sharecroppers. When I was six or seven, I got up at dawn to go to the cotton fields and help with the picking. I saw things I can't even talk about." He walked four or five miles to school every day, and by twelve he was milking the cows. At twenty, he followed his brother to New York City, arriving in the middle of the 1965 blackout.

"I was always cooking," he says. "Before I had a restaurant, I had a table in the park, then I had a food truck." His original restaurant was on 151st Street, a gathering place; rising rents and a bad landlord forced him out. He struggled to survive until he found the storefront on 132nd Street. From the food truck to his first restaurant to the current spot, the same customers have followed him.

Fried chicken master
Charles Gabriel, in his
kitchen.

"Harlem was the Black capital of America, and even decades after the original migration, there were still a lot of people from the South and their descendants," says Curtis Archer, who works for the Harlem Community Development Corporation and is often called the unofficial mayor of Harlem. "After a long night of partying, friends would all gather to break bread, often at soul food restaurants. This was comfort food," he adds. But these days, Harlem is changing fast, with new apartment buildings going up, fancy restaurants opening, millennials swooping in for the neighborhood's "new" cool. A friend points out that Harlem was always cool, but not for the millennials and realtors who have changed it so radically but who for many years were too scared to go that far uptown. After all, the first Starbucks opened in Harlem only in 1999.

"It's true that the Harlem food landscape has been completely altered since around 2000, when new eateries started opening and the historic landmarks started to shutter," Curtis tells me.

"A lot of young people now want to grab and go," adds Charles. A businessman as well as an acclaimed chef, he understands and is adapting to the new style. Even the sides he cooks to go with the chicken are now all vegetarian. (Do not despair! The mac 'n' cheese, the okra, the greens, the succotash are all rich and delicious.)

As it gets late, Charles and Curtis shoot the breeze about the Harlem they knew, the people they knew, the places they ate: Wilson's, Copeland's Reliable, Flash Inn. All gone, Curtis says. "It wasn't just about food but also community," he adds.

For dessert, there's homemade peach cobbler and rich banana pudding—Charles makes his own custard. Karen and I have now completely fallen off the wagon and given up any idea of sticking to our diets; Curtis never tried.

"It'd be great to see Charles's business expand," says Karen, putting down her spoon. She adds, "I don't believe the quality would ever suffer. As mild-mannered as he is, I can't see Charles tolerating that for one second! He's got so much pride for his product—so much love and respect for the community he feeds."

THE APOLLO THEATER

THE APOLLO THEATER on West 125th Street, red neon sign above, marquee lit up at night, crowds waiting excitedly, is as close to the heart of Harlem culturally—physically, too—as you can get. More than any other theater in New York, it delivers an ineluctable thrill as soon as you go inside. "Monumental," Smokey Robinson calls this legendary theater.

The lobby is not, at first, especially seductive—a long counter with souvenirs and books—but then, on your right, you come to a mural. When I met Robinson, he said, "Right there on the wall are people I grew up hearing about: Sammy Davis Jr., Sarah Vaughan, Count Basie, Duke Ellington, and of course, Ella Fitzgerald. When I made it on that wall, I felt we [he and his group, the Miracles] had made it, because the Apollo is the Apollo."

Inside the Apollo
dressing rooms.

In a thousand ways, the Apollo matters. It exudes history and culture and comedy and art. Head into the main auditorium, with its red plush seats and gilded boxes and balconies. Overhead are the chandeliers. Facing you is the stage. In 1934, this was where Ella Fitzgerald, a skinny seventeen-year-old girl, appeared during the first Apollo amateur night. Her dress was ragged. The audience—Apollo audiences were tough—booed the newcomer. Then she began to sing. She opened her mouth, and she was Ella Fitzgerald. Within six months, she was a star, the biggest thing in swing, knocking them dead up at Harlem's Savoy Ballroom.

From the outside, the theater looks much like any other large urban venue. Inside, though, you feel the life there, the performances, the anticipation, the famous amateur nights where careers were made— those of Ella, Sarah Vaughan, Michael Jackson. What Broadway was to white America, the Apollo was to the Black world.

When the neoclassical building designed by George Keister first opened in 1914, it was as a burlesque house. Harlem was still largely white. In 1933, Mayor Fiorello H. La Guardia cracked down on burlesque

Fans waiting to get into the Apollo, 1959.

shows, though, and in 1934, the theater was rededicated as a venue for variety revues. By that time, the population of Harlem was nearly 70 percent Black. The Apollo quickly became a center for the best in music, dance, and comedy. From Count Basie to Bill "Bojangles" Robinson to Jackie "Moms" Mabley, supremely talented performers began to take the stage.

Fast-forward nearly ninety years, and I'm here in the audience listening to Billy Mitchell, the resident historian and official tour guide for the Apollo—you can book one of his tours most days—who started working at the theater in 1965 when he was fifteen. He was hanging around the stage door when somebody asked if he'd go for coffee, and with that, he became a permanent fixture at the theater. Mitchell encourages young people in the audience to come on up to the stage and try performing. He urges them to rub the stump of an old elm tree on the stage, as every performer does, for good luck. The original elm stood on the sidewalk on Seventh Avenue between 131st and 132nd, known as the Boulevard of Dreams, between the august Lafayette Theatre and Connie's Inn (a nightclub where Louis Armstrong played); aspiring performers often gathered

around the tree. When the tree was cut down in 1934, its stump went to the Apollo.

After Mitchell recounts this legend, he takes us to see the wall of signatures started by the Apollo Theater's crew in the late 1980s. Look closely, and you can see that the wall has been signed by Tony Bennett, Barack and Michelle Obama, Bruce Springsteen, and many more.

Downstairs are the dressing rooms where Lena Horne and Billie Holiday got ready for their numbers, where Ella Fitzgerald played cards between performances, where James Brown got his famous cape ready.

Brown, who became a mentor to young Billy Mitchell, who told him to finish high school and go to college, recorded his most famous album in the theater. *James Brown Live at the Apollo*, generally considered one of the greatest albums of all time, was recorded in October 1962, the same week the Cuban Missile Crisis was unfolding. When he died, Brown was memorialized at the theater. The marquee sign read, "Rest in Peace Apollo Legend, the Godfather of Soul, James Brown, 1933–2006." Pallbearers carried the gold-plated casket inside and onto the stage, where mourners could pay their respects.

James Brown laid out in
his coffin for the viewing at
the Apollo.

Jazz writer Will Friedwald notes, "Just as the theater itself is in the geographical epicenter of Harlem, the Apollo has always been ground zero for every major development in Black vernacular music, from swing bands in the 1930s to bebop and R&B in the '40s, gospel and soul in the '50s and '60s, followed by funk, reggae, rap, hip-hop, and every sound that has come since."

For all its storied history, the Apollo is still a dynamic place, a theater with contemporary performers, where amateur night is ongoing, where plays are mounted. Recently there was a staged version of Ta-Nehisi Coates's *Between the World and Me*. The theater feels to me like the great anchor in a Harlem bursting with culture—the Studio Museum, the National Jazz Museum, the Harlem School of the Arts, the Schomburg Center, the Maysles Documentary Center. People say gentrification means the end of the real Harlem, but then people are always mourning what they knew instead of loving what's here. In Harlem, there's still a sense of community.

One Sunday, I go with friends to the Abyssinian Baptist Church, a few blocks north of the Apollo and another of Harlem's great anchors. I see this sense of community in the service, the congregants, the choir, the welcome to strangers.

Afterward, my friends and I meet my cousins for brunch at Ruby's Vintage on 137th Street and Adam Clayton Powell Jr. Boulevard. Before we even sit down, there are greetings and an exchange of news and gossip. All this gives the lie to the notion that New York City is not a welcoming place.

Harlem seems to me to have something of the ambiance Greenwich Village had when I was a kid. It feels somehow apart from the city, a separate village. I like it here. But after a lifetime downtown, I can't imagine quitting it; I'm planted down there for life and always have been. Downtown has the comfort, the ease, the cheer of the familiar; it's mine, and I love it. But to be honest, if I were starting out all over again, I think I might pull up roots and move to Harlem.

Amateur Night at the Apollo, 1940s.

APOLOGIES

I KNOW, I KNOW—I've left out scores, hundreds, thousands of places in New York City. Every time I'd make a list, friends would call up, irritated, insistent, passionate. There are almost no theaters in this thing, as more than one friend has noted. No Public Theater, no City Center, no Beacon. Where is Carnegie Hall? Where is Radio City Music Hall, that last of the great movie and show palaces, where the annual Christmas Spectacular was the thrill of my tiny life when I was a kid? I mean, come on!! You left out the Cherry Lane Theatre, and all of Broadway and off Broadway! Huh?! Where is Lincoln Center?! The Metropolitan Opera, where I first saw *Carmen* at the age of six? But what about . . . ? What about . . . ?

What about the Crosby Street Hotel? No P. J. Clarke's? No Joe Allen? Or Joe's Pub? Are you insane?! No Balthazar? (I did write another book about that one.) No sushi, no pizza? No pizza! (The best pizza is, alas, in that *other* borough.)

How about the knish man? The Indian spice guy? Veniero's pastry? You're not putting in the Union Square Greenmarket?! Bigelow's drugstore, where Walt Whitman shopped, or the Frick, or the Studio Museum?

So many places, so little space, but let's at least give due to Cookshop, the first farm-to-table eatery where you could nosh on great food and also learn the name of your cow and her farmer. And Beatrice's, aka Il Posto Accanto, maybe the best wine bar in the city, with absolutely the ne plus ultra spaghetti vongole. Not to mention Ground Support, where I have coffee most mornings.

Because you are either a New Yorker or a New York lover, you'll be using much stronger language when you complain, What about Jack's Wife Freda? And you must think I'm a real knuckledragger to have omitted the Juilliard school and its concerts. And Marcus Samuelsson's Red Rooster. And B&H, the only place to shop for electronics, because they actually talk to you and take their time (I even buy Apple stuff there); and Frenchette, Lee Hanson and Riad Nasr's restaurant; and the Frenchette bakery, which reminds us there are new things that make the city worthwhile, especially if they sell maple brioche and pear Danish.

No comedy, or ballet, or folk music at Town Hall? No dance clubs? Well, I don't dance much, so I'm sorry. I apologize. You're right. I even left out Bergdorf's.

The places in this book are the places I love, my personal favorites, restaurants or shops that have history for me and that seem to me evidence that New York is still alive, that it is still the real thing.

You want to argue about it? Well, it's a New Yorker's favorite pastime—at least when we're not eating.

ACKNOWLEDGMENTS

THERE ARE AN awful lot of people to thank, some for the book itself, some for coming up with places to include, others for taking part in the eating and drinking and walking that are the only way to cover Manhattan. So . . .

Thanks first to Lia Ronnen and Bridget Monroe Itkin at Artisan for commissioning the book mostly on good faith and a few hours of conversation; and to Bridget for her elegant editing and for putting up with me. Elise Ramsbottom did a sensational job in helping to pull the photos together. Thank you also to Nina Simoneaux, Sibylle Kazeroid, Judith Sutton, David Schiller, Annie O'Donnell, Suet Chong, Nancy Murray, Erica Huang, and the rest of the team at Artisan for turning out a beautiful book.

To William Clark, my agent, for taking me to them.

To Hanya Yanagihara for commissioning the 212 column at the *Times*, and for listening to my endless and probably endlessly repetitive tales of New York City; and to my friend Salman Rushdie for coming up with the perfect title for it. To Alice Newell-Hanson at the *Times* for her perfect and patient editing, and Betsy Horan, also at the *Times*, for the great picture editing. Nina Westervelt took many of the photographs and has become a valued friend.

For advice, suggestions, and help with the actual eating and drinking and general survival in what have been some weird times: Sally Roy, Peter Nelson, Dick Robinson, Vladimir Pozner, Billy Di Michelle, Lynne Uy, Gene Uy, Mike Gilsenan, Curtis Archer, Karen Murray,

Dawn Delbanco, Yvonne Delbanco, Emilia Hermann, Rona Middleberg, Steven Zwerling, Melissa Middleberg, Jane Mushabac, Margo Jefferson, Dubi Leshem, Justine Haemmerlie, Rosie Rodricks, Caite Panzer, John Panzer, Paul Solman, Peter Kazaras, Steven Wagner, Navina Haidar, Martin Rosenbaum, Jill Evans, Frank Wynne, Rocky Ahimaz, Steve Barr, Shaun Woodward, Luke Redgrave, Gene Farone, Paul Eshkenazi, and all the people who own and work at the shops, cafés, bars, and restaurants in this book, who spent hours with me, answering questions, recounting family histories, telling New York tales, pouring Negronis, and just being generally terrific—many of them are already in the book.

PHOTOGRAPHY CREDITS

ALL IMAGES IN this book were provided by the business owners, with the exception of the below. Artisan has made every effort to secure permission and provide appropriate credit wherever possible for all images in the book. If you believe a credit to be incorrect or missing, we would appreciate notification.

Page 2: Andreas Feininger/Getty Images

Pages 6–7: Spencer Platt/Getty Images

Pages 10 and 14: Reggie Nadelson

Page 17: Nina Westervelt

Page 21: Daniel Krieger

Page 24: Paul Quitorian

Pages 28–34: Paul Quitorian

Pages 36, 38, and 41: Nina Westervelt

Pages 44–46: Nina Westervelt

Page 47: Courtesy of the James Brown House

Pages 50 (right) and 51: Adam Friedberg

Pages 54, 55, 58, and 59: Nina Westervelt

Pages 62–64: Emily Andrews

Page 68: Robin Holland

Page 70: Artwork by George Griffin

Pages 75 and 76 (left): Paul Quitorian

Page 80: Nina Westervelt

Page 82: Christophe L. Smith

Pages 83–85: Nina Westervelt

Page 90: *Untitled (Julius')* (detail) from *Night Music* 2019/Ian Lewandowski

Page 93: Fred W. McDarrah/Getty Images

Page 96: Jack Vartoogian/Getty Images

Page 97: Sam Falk/New York Times Co./Getty Images

Page 99: Hemis/Alamy Stock Photo

Pages 102 and 107: Charissa Fay

Pages 110–113 and 117: Nina Westervelt

Pages 114–115: Mark Higashino

Page 116: Roxanne Lowit

Pages 120 and 121: Matthew Cylinder

Page 132: Gustavo Caballero/Getty Images for SOBEWFF

Page 133: Squire Fox

Page 136: Shimon and Tammar

Pages 139 and 142–143: Daniel Krieger

Pages 154 and 158–159: Paul Quitorian

Page 157 (left): Reggie Nadelson

Page 160: Jamie Maletz

Pages 168 and 171–173: Paul Quitorian

Pages 176, 179 (left), and 181: Nina Westervelt

Pages 182 and 185: Heather Sten

Page 188: Nina Westervelt

Page 190: Album/Alamy Stock Photo

Pages 192–194: Nina Westervelt

Page 198 (left): Historic Collection/Alamy Stock Photo

Page 202–206: Nina Westervelt

Page 208: Rob Stephenson

Page 210: Steve Schapiro/Corbis via Getty Images

Page 211: PoPsie Randolph/Michael Ochs Archives/Getty Image

Page 212: Everett Collection Inc/Alamy Stock Photo

Pages 214–215: Herbert Gehr/The LIFE Picture Collection via Getty Images

Page 216: rblfmr/Shutterstock.com

Page 219: Peter Stackpole/The LIFE Picture Collection via Getty Images

Page 220: Nina Westervelt

Page 224: NY Daily News Archive via Getty Images